Celebrating

Women

DATE DUE

MAR 1 7 1999		
SEP 0 8 2000		
OCT 0 4 2000		
NOV 2 5 2001		
FEB 1 7 2009		
FEB 2 6 2015		
FEB 2 9 2016		

242
CEL Celebrating women

DEMCO

THE NEW EDITION

Edited by Hannah Ward, Jennifer Wild & Janet Morley

Celebrating Women

MOREHOUSE PUBLISHING

HARRISBURG, PA

First published in Great Britain 1995
Society for Promoting Christian Knowledge

First U.S. Edition published by

MOREHOUSE PUBLISHING
Editorial Office
871 Ethan Allen Highway
Ridgefield, CT 06877

Corporate Office
P.O. Box 1321
Harrisburg, PA 17105

Library of Congress Cataloging-in-Publication Data

    Celebrating women / edited by Hannah Ward, Jennifer Wild,
Janet Morley.
       p.   cm.
    ISBN 0-8192-1652-6
       1. Prayers. 2. Feminist theology—Miscellanea. 3. Women
in the Anglican Communion—Miscellanea. I. Ward, Hannah.
II. Wild, Jennifer. III. Morley, Janet.
BV245.C395 1995
242' .643—dc20

                            95-24925
                               CIP

Printed in the United States of America

CONTENTS

Reclaiming the Word 31

Bone of my Bone 71

This is my Body   94

Breaking Through 114

Taste and See 130

Blessings 146

Gathered Together 152

Perhaps it is no wonder that women were first at the Cradle and last at the Cross. They had never known a man like this man — there has never been such another. A prophet and teacher who never nagged at them, never flattered or coaxed or patronised; who never made arch jokes about them, never treated them either as 'The women, God help us' or 'The ladies, God bless them!'; who rebuked without querulousness and praised without condescension; who took their questions and arguments seriously; who never mapped out their sphere for them, never urged them to be feminine or jeered at them for being female; who had no axe to grind and no uneasy male dignity to defend; who took them as he found them and was completely unselfconscious. There is no act, no sermon, no parable in the whole Gospel that borrows its pungency from female perversity; nobody could possibly guess from the words and deeds of Jesus that there was anything 'funny' about woman's nature.

But we might easily deduce it from His contemporaries, and from His prophets before Him, and from His Church to this day. Women are not human; nobody shall persuade us that they are human; let them say what they like, we will not believe it, though One rose from the dead.

Dorothy L. Sayers

The first edition of *Celebrating Women* was brought out in 1986 by Women in Theology and the Movement for the Ordination of Women as a piece of 'barefoot publishing', beautifully designed but produced at minimal cost. The editors were convinced that the energies of the women's movement were flowing strongly within the churches as well as in the rest of society, but established religious publishers were cautious about the existence of any sort of market for women's liturgical writing.

The years since its publication have revealed a wealth of interest in women's spirituality and we hope that *Celebrating Women* made a contribution to that, inspiring more women to start articulating their faith in fresh and distinctive ways.

This new and much expanded edition bears witness to a wave of creativity. It has been created quite simply by calling for recently written material for a new edition, either from the original authors or through the same networks that promoted *Celebrating Women* initially. The response was astonishing, and we decided to do no further searching for material, first because we could not remotely include everything we were sent, in any case, but also because we wanted to reflect faithfully the community of women who had been actively touched by the original edition.

All of that collection is retained in the new edition, including the original section headings. We found that there was plenty of new material which naturally fitted into these categories. In particular the biblical section 'Reclaiming the Word' filled up quite quickly. Contributors have clearly found great energy in exploring biblical stories about women which until the last decade have received little attention. We also received a good deal of material which explores spirituality through experiences distinctive to women (but until recently not deemed to be a suitable – or even a possible – source of religious insight): childbirth, menstruation and female sexuality.

But further sections have been added to the original

list, because of the new feel of some of the material we considered. In the original *Celebrating Women* there was a fair bit of (justified) lamenting by women about our situation in society and in the churches. There is still plenty to lament about, but much of the new material has shed any sense of helplessness or paralysed introspection. The awareness of pain has moved into a constructive anger or a clear-sighted analysis, and there is a growing and healthy tone of resilience, decisiveness and authority – a sense that necessary changes have been made or that a real transition is happening. This is reflected in the new section 'Breaking Through'. And there is a good deal of sheer delight in the new section we have called 'Taste and See'. We are struck by the amazing variety of ways of speaking about God that have been unleashed, once the adequacy of exclusively patriarchal language has been questioned. These prayers and poems are poignant, imaginative, tough – and sometimes funny. New 'orthodoxies' of women's spirituality (like circle dancing!) are not themselves allowed to become pompous or absolute.

We noticed also some interesting trends in the content and form of the material offered, as well as in its tone. The years of struggle within the Church of England for the ordination of women to the priesthood are reflected in a variety of ways. There are poems and prayers by women looking to ordination, but there is also a wealth of material arising out of the non-eucharistic, experimental symbolic liturgies that women have developed in the interim. Some of these show the influence of recent interest in the older traditional religions that underlie our Christian culture. While for some women the important movement in recent years has been towards inclusion or simple acceptance within the structures of church authority, for others those structures have come to have less centrality or even relevance.

But one important movement towards inclusive language has been deliberately to work within the disciplines of the very traditional literary forms of

Christian liturgy: collects, psalms, eucharistic prayers and hymns. As in the first edition, we have selected a mixture of formal material suitable for corporate worship, and less structured pieces for individual reading or informal group reflection.

Many prayers in the first edition reflected the concerns and activities of women within the peace movement during the 1980s. Issues of justice and major world events also feature in many of the new prayers and poems: the Gulf War, the impact of AIDS, environmental concerns, the recession, and the persistence of poverty in a world of widening divisions between rich and poor.

It is heartening to see that women are shedding our hesitancy and inclination to self-apology when writing about our perceptions of God. But it is even more crucial that as writers we should not fall back – albeit with a 'feminine' feel to it – into that dominant form of spirituality in our culture which is purely private, personal and interior. For this reason, we are glad to include some strong corporate confessions which make it clear that women cannot take refuge in any sort of political innocence.

Finally, it is worth asking what impact women's new ways of writing, thinking, enacting and praying our faith have had or are likely to have. We discern quite a shift since 1986 in the consciousness of how some kinds of religious language have hurt and excluded women. And there is much interest and debate (not only among women) about how things could be different – along with an awareness of the pitfalls, inelegancies of language and potential doctrinal problems that can arise. Certainly it is now generally the case that it feels uncomfortable not to add 'and women' when 'men' are referred to in church. Practice has changed in this respect.

However, very recent developments such as the new Roman Catholic Catechism (with its deliberate decision to overturn inclusive translations and to re-introduce even more 'men' than were originally present) suggest a backlash. As far as different ways of speaking about God are concerned, churches have been more cautious anyway, but relentlessly male language is at least regarded by many as problematic. Many anthologies and official denominational prayer books have looked to women's new writing for texts that inspire. The contributions that come from outside the UK, particularly those from Aotearoa/New Zealand, reflect a stage of development well ahead of the situation in the UK.

With so many more women now taking full authority within church structures, it will be interesting in the future to see whether inclusive language becomes more widely acceptable, or, by contrast, is kept firmly at the fringes of the churches, if those women want to be perceived as traditional bearers of authority. But for the contributors to this anthology, and for many more, we suspect that after opening such a floodgate for prayer, there will be no going back.

Janet Morley, Jennifer Wild, Hannah Ward
June 1994

'Christians are formed by the way in which they pray.'

So reads the preface to the Alternative Service Book of the Church of England. The language we use has an enormous power to shape our perceptions: of ourselves, of our world, and of God. However, we inherit a language for worship which, whether we are speaking of human beings or of God, overwhelmingly uses masculine pronouns and metaphors, as if these were neutral in their effect on those who pray. 'All men' are encouraged to seek 'brotherhood' with their 'fellow men'. And God is always 'He'; not surprisingly, 'He' is frequently addressed with titles that are very male (not to say macho) in flavour: King, Judge, Almighty, Lord of Hosts (i.e. Armies).

Increasingly, it is being recognized that this usage creates difficulties for women. In entering the traditional discourse of prayer, however nourishing it may be in other ways, as women we experience ourselves as absent, invisible, anomalous, even alien. At best, women must make a continuous act of translation, in order to find ourselves included in a male-oriented discourse; for many, such an activity is an irritation and a distraction from worship; and for a growing number of women, to be surrounded by exclusive language is a repeated encounter with rejection, precisely in the place where we seek acceptance at the deepest level of our being.

Exclusive language is not a trivial matter, in church or out of it. It is both an accurate symptom of women's actual exclusion from many central forms of ministry and decision-making; and it is also a means of continually re-creating the attitudes which support such exclusion as 'normal', or within the purposes of God. Women can participate in this language, and speak the words that erase us, or we can choose to remain silent. Alternatively, we can struggle to create a language that includes us. *Celebrating Women* reflects the re-vision and new articulation of Christian truth that is being undertaken from the perspective of women. In this process, there is both pain and celebration; and there is an exploratory 'feel' to many of the pieces, which suggests that some of the hidden insights of women are only beginning to be expressed.

The book is divided into five main sections. 'Out of the Depths' contains two kinds of material. Some echoes the traditional psalm of lament, to express the depths of the particular pain that women experience in our culture. Other pieces seek to explore the nature of God through imagery that is unfamiliar: images of the feminine, of chaos, darkness, and 'depths' are explored as unknown aspects of ourselves where we may experience God.

'Reclaiming the Word' includes examples of how women are rereading the Bible in the light of our experience. The Bible has historically been used both as a source for patriarchal attitudes, and a force for liberation from them. Women are currently exploring how different kinds of biblical text can be usable and inspiring for us. Stories about women have received particular attention, since these have often been used, in the church's tradition, to reinforce assumptions about the limited place of women as disciples or bearers of faith.

'Bone of my Bone' is a section in which confession and intercession are interwoven. Women are no more 'innocent' of the sin of sexism than are men, though we have borne different and greater costs. Nevertheless women, through collusion and manipulation, do help to maintain structural sin in all its forms. Our participation needs to be named, along with our willingness and strength to be involved in a worldwide struggle for justice. Some of the pieces are particularly appropriate for mixed groups, some for women only.

'This is my Body' is a section of eucharistic prayers and material suitable for worship around a meal. It is notable that in many parts of the church, women are excluded from presiding at the symbolic meal. Serving food, however, is a feature of our everyday life so common as to go unnoticed. These prayers affirm women's daily eucharistic activity and, in this context, they speak of our personal and political brokenness, but also of our joy and power.

In 'Gathered Together', we offer some suggestions about how to create an act of worship together as a group. We give an example of a liturgy devised by a particular group of women [now on p. 109 of this edition]. Individual pieces of writing need somehow to be owned by the group that uses them; it will be seen that many of the items throughout the booklet were written for specific occasions, in the context of a worshipping group of women. We hope that the material in *Celebrating Women* will not only be reused, but will encourage other women to find their own words for worship.

In offering these words for use, both for group occasions and for private meditation, there is no suggestion of wanting to replace words or images that continue to create meaning for women. Still less are we proposing that these words are in any sense adequate. All language with which we address God is fundamentally inadequate to the task, and needs to be abandoned when it gets in the way of worship rather than assisting it. The provisional nature of all worship material applies to this selection as to others; but our concern is that women should be enabled to seek that silence before God which is beyond words, rather than settle for the silence of the inarticulate.

Janet Morley, Hannah Ward
September 1986

1   A prayer to the Trinity

Beloved God,
In you we live and move and have our being.

Jesus, Liberator,
with you we walk the way of love.

Creator Spirit,
through you we are made one.

God, trinity of love, we seek you in the dance of life.
We embrace your love.
We would dance.

This is the meaning of the resurrection, that we can
    dance.

Kathy
Galloway   Alleluia. Amen.

2   Come to the living God

Come to the living God,
    Come to stand alongside the poor.
    Come to struggle with those who seek freedom.
Jan   Come to resist all that offends God's justice.
Berry   Come to the living, disturbing God.

3   God of the poor

God of the poor,
we long to meet you
yet almost miss you;
we strive to help you
yet only discover our need.

Interrupt our comfort
with your nakedness,
touch our possessiveness
with your poverty,
and surprise our guilt
Janet   with the grace of your welcome
Morley   in Jesus Christ. Amen.

⁴   **Epiphany prayer**

God of the light and of the darkness,
open our eyes to the signs of failure
      which reveal your presence
open our ears to your words
      spoken in unexpected places
open our hearts to your love
      shown towards us by those you have sent
      to share our lives.
May our worship not interrupt true worship of you
may our agendas not leave out the Kingdom of God
Kirsty   may our planning not separate our confidence from
Thorpe   faith.

⁵   **Centring prayer**

Come weave a silence to my ears
Come weave a resting to my eyes
Jan   Come still the troubling of my heart
Hughes   And at this day's ending, come.

6   **Meditation with silence**

In stillness
And silence
I know
You are my God
And I love you

silence

There is no
Felt awareness
But deeper inside
Than I knew existed
I am with you

silence

All else
Is of no account
My pride, self-doubt
Inhibitions
Washed aside

silence

Held in being
Loved into life
Delicately balanced
Joy transcending
Aching anguish

silence

Called by name
Compelled by love
Desiring nothing
Christine   Except your will
Bull   Expressed in me

7   **Spirit of God**

Spirit of God,
brooding over the waters
of our chaos,
inspire us to
generous living.

Wind of God,
dancing over the desert
of our reluctance,
lead us to the oasis
of celebration.

Breath of God,
inspiring communication
among strangers,
Kate   make us channels
McIlhagga   of your peace.

8   **Let down your hearts**

Extract from a   Let down your hearts
Women In   **We let them down to God.**
Theology liturgy

Humble God,
We have looked for you in the heavens,
and talked to you in complex religious abstracts;
We have believed that we will understand your
    purposes
by listening to the high and the mighty;
We have aspired to progress, the raising of
    standards,
we have wanted bigger and better:

Draw our hearts and minds inward and downward
     to you,
who became nothing for love of us,
so that we may live our lives in simple reality.
Amen.

Let us go down to the core,
to the earth's core,
where the fire will consume
the dross of our religion,
where only the flame of hope can burn.
Let us go down to the depths,
to the ocean's deeps,
where the weight of water will compress
the airiness of our theology,
Alison   where only the blind see
Norris   and only the deaf hear.

9   Spirit of comfort and longing

Spirit of comfort and longing,
enfold my fear,
unclothe me of my pride,
unweave my thoughts,
uncomplicate my heart,
and give me surrender:
that I may tell my wounds,
Janet   lay down my work,
Morley   and greet the dark.

10 **A story of creation**

Once upon a time, in the beginning,
a labour of love was undertaken.

It started with a sign, to show that
something was about to happen.
Light came forth from the deep
darkness, bright, clear and
unmistakable.
And it was very good.

At the second time, the waters were
broken. At first, they gushed, then
they dried to a trickle, and a space
was created. It was exactly the right
size. By now, the creation was well
under way.
And it was very good.

At the third time, a cradle was made
ready. It was comfortable and
beautiful and waiting. And food was
prepared, issuing sweetly and warmly
and in precisely the right measure
from the being of the labourer.
And it was very good.

At the fourth time, rhythm was
established. Ebbing and flowing,
contracting and expanding, pain and
joy, sun and moon, beginning and
ending. The labour of love
progressed.
And it was very good.

At the fifth time, there was
ceaseless activity. Fluttering like the
wings of the dove, humming like the
murmur of the dragonfly, swimming

like the darting golden fish,
wriggling like the lithe serpent,
leaping like the flashing deer,
surging like the mighty lion.
And it was very good.

At the sixth time, there was a
momentary, endless hesitation. Then
a child was born. And the child
looked just like the one who had
given it life. The child too was born
with the power to create and to make
decisions, and to love.
The labourer looked at all that had
been accomplished, and rejoiced, for
it was very good.

At the seventh time, the labour was
finished. The task was complete. And
Kathy the labourer rested, for she was very,
Galloway very tired.

11   **God our Lover**

God our Lover

You draw us to search for you;
you give us clues to your presence in creation;
we find you in each other's faces,
in the challenge and the intimacy of human love.
Yet always you elude our grasp;
familiar and yet always strange,
you both comfort and disturb our lives.
We surrender all our images of you,
and offer ourselves to your darkness;
that you may enable us to become your likeness
Janet more than we can imagine or conceive.
Morley Amen.

¹² **Bringing forth the Word**

Voice 1

From 'Magnificat',
a service of
rejoicing for the
work and witness
of women
throughout the
ages, Durham
Cathedral, 30
April 1983.
I heard a cry, like a woman in labour, a scream like a
woman bearing her first child.

Voice 2
Be merciful to me, Lord, for I am in trouble; my eyes
are tired from so much crying; I am completely worn
out. I am exhausted by sorrow. All my enemies and
especially my neighbours treat me with contempt.
(Psalm 31.9–11)

And the Word became flesh.

Voice 1
Lord, I am ridiculed and scorned all the time because I
proclaim your message. But when I say 'I will forget
the Lord and no longer speak in his name' then your
message is like a fire burning deep within me. I
try my best to hold it in but I can no longer keep it
back.
(Jeremiah 20.7, 9)

And the Word became flesh.

Voice 2
You, Lord, have made us cry out as a woman in labour
cries out in pain, we were in pain and agony, but we
gave birth to nothing. We have won no victory for our
land; we have accomplished nothing.
(Isaiah 26.17–18)

And the Word became flesh.

Voice 3
My holy city is like a woman who suddenly gives
birth to a child without ever going into labour. Has
anyone ever seen or heard of such a thing? Zion
will not have to suffer long before the nation is born.

Do not think that I will bring my nation to the point
of birth and not let them be born.
(Isaiah 66.7–9)

Voices 1, 2 & 3
For we know that up to the present times all of
creation groans with pain, like the pain of childbirth.
(Romans 8.22)

And the Word became flesh and dwelt among us.

¹³   **For the darkness of waiting**

From Liturgy of
Hope, Canterbury
Cathedral, 18
April 1986.

For the darkness of waiting
of not knowing what is to come
of staying ready and quiet and attentive,
we praise you O God

**For the darkness and the light
are both alike to you.**

For the darkness of staying silent
for the terror of having nothing to say
and for the greater terror of needing to say nothing,
we praise you O God

**For the darkness and the light
are both alike to you.**

For the darkness of loving
in which it is safe to surrender
to let go of our self-protection
and to stop holding back our desire,
we praise you O God

**For the darkness and the light
are both alike to you.**

For the darkness of choosing
when you give us the moment to speak, and act, and
　　change,
and we cannot know what we have set in motion,
but we still have to take the risk,
we praise you O God

**For the darkness and the light
are both alike to you.**

For the darkness of hoping
in a world which longs for you,
for the wrestling and the labouring of all creation
for wholeness and justice and freedom,
we praise you O God

Janet　**For the darkness and the light**
Morley　**are both alike to you.**

14　　**The Other**

Whatever I find if I search will be wrong.
I must wait: sternest trial of all, to contain myself,
Sit passive, receptive, and patient, empty
Of every demand and desire, until
That other, that being I never would have found
Though I spent my whole life in the quest, will step
Clear of the shadows, approach like a wild, awkward
　　child.

And this will be the longest task: to attend,
To open myself. To still my energy
Is harder than to use it in any cause.
Yet surely she will only be revealed
By pushing against the grain of my ardent nature
That always yearns for choice. I feel it painful
And strong as a birth in which there is no pause.

I must hold myself back from every lure of action
To let her come closer, a wary smile on her face,
One arm lifted: to greet me or ward off attack —
I cannot decipher that uncertain gesture.
I must even control the pace of my breath
Until she has drawn her circle near enough
To capture the note of her faint reedy voice.

And then as in dreams, when a language unspoken
Since times before childhood is recalled (when
I was as timid as she, my forgotten sister —
Her presence my completion and reward), I begin
To understand, in fragments, the message she waited
So long to deliver. Loving her I shall learn
My own secret at last from the words of her song.

Ruth
Fainlight

¹⁵ **Out of the depths**

Out of the depths I cry to you, O God,
Hear my voice, O God, listen to my pleading.

My voice is weak, O God, my God,
Although it speaks for many.
It is the voice of Sarah, shamed before her servant,
Barren, and given no worth.
It is the voice of Hagar, abused by her mistress,
Driven out into the desert with her child.
It is the voice of Rachel, weeping for her children,
Weeping, for they are all dead.
It is the voice of Mary, robbed of her humanity,
Woman, yet not woman.
It is the voice of Martha, taught to be a servant,
Challenged to choose for herself.
It is the voice of a nameless woman, bought and sold,
Then given back to herself.

It is the voice of women, groaning in labour,
Sweating in toil, abandoned in hardship,

Weeping in mourning, awakened in worry,
Enslaved in dependency, afraid of their weakness.

Do you hear my voice, O God, my God?
Can you answer me?
The words I hear all speak to me of men.
You said I am also in your image,
You are my father, are you also mother,
Comfort-bringing like the loving arms?

Do you hear my voice, O God, my God?
Can you answer me?
I can sing your song of praise no longer,
I am not at home in this world any more.
My heart is full of tears for my sisters,
They choke my words of joy.

Do you hear my voice, O God, my God?
Can you answer me?
You sent your son, a man, to love me,
But him they killed also.

Kathy What is the new life that you promise me?
Galloway *I do not want more of the same.*

16 **Reclaiming Halloween: remembering the victims of
the witch-hunts**

This service was
first used by a
women's
spirituality group
in the University
of Guelph,
Ontario, Canada,
at Halloween
1991.

Introduction

Litany for voices

Halloween, the time when children learn through play
        that devils, witches, darkness, fear belong together.
The time when we recall the thousands upon thousands
        who were burned to death as witches, most of
        them women.
Who were these 'witches'?
What was their crime?

Some said No to the church's teaching that women
    were evil and should suffer.
Some found divinity in Mother Earth, and kept alive
    her worship.
Some gathered secretly to worship outside the iron
    confines of the church.

But many were simply victims of a terrifying,
    murderous process.
Many were arrested and burned on the forced
    confessions of others, broken by torture.
Their crimes were fiction, conjured up by twisted minds
    in priestly power.
Stripped of everything – clothing, dignity, family,
    justice – they were destroyed.

For generation after generation, over four hundred
    years, the innocent were condemned, womanpower
    was brutally crushed, and a gentle spirituality of
    the earth was burned out.

Today we remember,
    with a horror that such things could happen;
    with a rage that fills us with the furies of old;
    with a sorrow that knows this cannot be undone;
    with fearfulness of the violence which goes on.
We gather to mourn the holocaust of women.

Music for meditation, and readings

Ritual to reclaim

*For example, stripping a pumpkin of its witch's hat,
mask, etc., and placing it with a collection of autumn
leaves and fruit.*

Prayer

Grandmother God, we honour you as Holy Crone,
Ancient Wisdom, spinning and weaving the strands of
    new life.
Grandmother God, we find your face in the dark
    mysteries of the earth, the womb, the wild places.
Grandmother God, we call upon you to blow on the
    embers of our womanspirit, and make us leap and burn
    with life.

Let us join with our sisters, the persecuted, the
dominated, the violated, and say
    Never again,
    never again,
    never again. **Amen.**

Lucy
Reid   Closing music

17   **Broken**

Broken
by the wheel of the car
driving me to the next
appointment

Broken
by the tearing tensions
of demanding opposing
compartments of my life

Broken
by the fall
from the pedestal
on which I chose to stand

Broken
by disappointment
of those who thought me
strong and sure

Broken
by impermeable silence
unseen waves of mute resistance
from life denying loss

Broken
by words of bitterness
and hatred
spewed from a dark
and unimagined
place within

Broken
by angry taunts
of those who would not hear
my fear full words

Broken
the glass-like
clarity of vision
into a thousand jagged
frosty fragments
splintering the ground

Broken
steadfastly
as bread is broken
broken to be shared
among us

Jean   Broken
Clark   to be healed

¹⁸ Pain

Pain is a swift, silent invader.
In a fraction of a second
he storms through years of hard won self restraint,
knocking over ego defences like so many skittles,
slicing through the barbed wire of control
                              with cool precision.
SAS trained he is. Brutal.
He forces us, ashen-faced, to admit our torturing
                              incompleteness,
till we scream for the healing touch
                    of a merciful, mothering God.
Then softly he slips away, slowly, silently
                              into the shadows.

Mary Hanrahan

¹⁹ Bed and breakfast

I live sheltered by the name
For a cheap holiday.
Some holiday. A family of slugs
Lives in the bathroom, mice scurry
Grey as fear. There is the occasional
Rat. But what I mind most is being
Squashed with the children in one room,
Loving, fighting, eating, sleeping
Publicly; queuing to use facilities
Stained by others' existence.
So, I have a roof. Must I be always
Thankful for small mercies?
What I want is a home.
Sod your trickle down economy,
The only thing that trickles here is
Rain, relentlessly through the ceiling.
Trickle, God, can't you send a flood,
Justice in torrents to carry me to my
Dream home? Nothing elaborate: just

Damp-free, no fungus in the corners;
The only creatures there present by
Ann   Invitation; water running through pipes;
Lewin   Space, privacy. Not much to ask.

²⁰   **The women of Jerusalem weep for Jesus**

From Stations of   Daughters of Jerusalem,
the Cross : Iona   sisters once summoned to watch over the sleep of
1991.   lovers,
                     how often have you wept for men,
                     yet stayed dry-eyed and silent
                     in your own pain?

                     Can you know blessing in fertility
                     when the axe is laid to the root of the green world?
                     Can you know joy in childbirth
                     when you are bearing down,
                     bearing your children into calamity?
                     Can you know grace in giving suck
                     when they are taking the children's food
                     and selling it for the dogs of war?

                     Daughters of Jerusalem,
                     sisters once summoned to watch over the sleep of
                          lovers,
Alison   weep not now for me,
Norris   weep for yourselves and for your children.

²¹   **The desert**

                     The desert waits,
                     ready for those who come,
                     who come obedient to the Spirit's leading;
                     or who are driven,
                     because they will not come any other way.

The desert always waits,
ready to let us know who we are –
the place of self-discovery.

And whilst we fear, and rightly,
the loneliness and emptiness and harshness,
we forget the angels,
whom we cannot see for our blindness,
but who come when God decides
that we need their help;
Ruth   when we are ready
Burgess   for what they can give us.

22   **The Crack**

There is a
crack
jagged and
long and
very deep.
The crack
is bleeding
having been torn
a howl
comes from its
heart
how to get back
together
with the proper fit
in right
relationship

the sides will not dovetail   neatly into place
too much of the edges   having crumbled away
nor can they   be forced together
without killing the fragile   flowers that cling to them
the crack   is permanent

one must, however, stand   on either side
as if it were not there   (although it is)
        (knowing it is)   within the good
    loving the other   in its absence
    whichever side it is   embracing it
        without that   crucial, agonizing coupling
            there is   only
the barren landscape   of despair
the blackened   territory of madness
            trust the crack
            it wants to be
        a wild luxuriant valley
            with waterfalls
        a river running through
            and on either side
Kathy   fertile   fruitful
Galloway   lands.

23   **God of Mystery**

God of Mystery,
whose silent depths arise encompassing me;
whose unknown, unknowable face hides from me;
Rebecca   clothe me in your darkest chasm
Nichol   tenderly.

24   **Psalm 51 A woman's Miserere**

Have mercy on me, O Life-giver, through your
        goodness,
In your great tenderness soothe away my faults;
Cleanse me of my guilt,
do not hold my failures against me.

For I have come to see that I fail you,
when I have not acknowledged with my whole being
that I am made truly in your image;
in not walking in your ways,
I have sinned against you.

You are love and truth itself,
and seek sincerity of heart;
teach me the secrets of wisdom.
Cleanse me from all that prevents me
from listening to your word.

Let me cry out with joy and gladness;
Leave behind me feelings of inferiority.
Do not hold it against me
that I have fallen in with men's distortions.

Creator, call forth a willing response from me;
infuse in me a new spirit of confidence;
Let me be aware of your presence,
and draw strength from your Spirit.

Giver of life, source of salvation,
Let me rejoice in serving you.
Keep my spirit responsive to you,
and I shall show forth to the sexist
the true way to you.

Save me from everlasting death, O God my Saviour,
and I shall acclaim your goodness.
Creator, give me the courage to speak forth your truth,
and use all my being, body, mind and soul,
to give you praise.

You call for a contrite heart:
the placatory sacrifices on the altars did not please you.
Our sacrifice is to do your will,
to work unceasingly for the coming of your realm.

Show forth your love to the women you have created;
guide us in building true community.

Ianthe Let the evils of dualism and domination be vanquished,
Pratt and a new age come where all live out your love.

²⁵   **Roll back the stone**

(Mark 16.1–8)

When we are all despairing;
when the world is full of grief;
when we see no way ahead,
    and hope has gone away:

Roll back the stone.

Although we fear change;
although we are not ready;
although we'd rather weep
    and run away:

Roll back the stone.

Because we're coming with the women;
because we hope where hope is vain;
because you call us from the grave
    and show the way:

Janet
Morley **Roll back the stone.**

26 **Prayer at a funeral**

O God who brought us to birth,
and in whose arms we die:
in our grief and shock
contain and comfort us;
embrace us with your love,
give us hope in our confusion,
Janet and grace to let go into new life,
Morley through Jesus Christ. Amen.

27   **A litany for many voices**

I am Eve.
I took the apple.
Adam ate it too
but I got all the blame.

I am Sarah.
Like many a wife
I packed and followed
obedient to his call,
not mine.

I Miriam, prophetess,
with a timbrel danced and sang.
Led the women celebrating –
Sisters, join our dance.

Samson was strong
but my guile was stronger,
I am Delilah.

I have no name but Jephthah's daughter.
He sacrificed me to his cruel god.
O mourn with me
my lost virginity.

I am Jezebel of ill-renown,
trampled by horses, eaten by dogs,
but I painted my eyes and adorned my head
and met death wearing my crown.

I, Vashti, knew my worth,
refused to come at a royal command,
so threatening all men on earth.

I am Judith, eloquent and wise,
who did not consider my own life
but God-empowered took my knife
and hacked off Holofernes' head.

I am old and brown.
From womb to grave I have
mothered and mourned
for I am Naomi the wise.
I discerned in Ruth a love unknown.

I am Anna.
I knew what to say.
I did not keep silent in the temple.
I knew God when I saw him and said so.

I am Martha,
who set the table, got the tea
and served Jesus and Mary.
It's hard to be left to work alone.

I am woman about to be stoned.
I dared to take a lover.
I saw man-faces angry and threatening.
Jesus the man looked in the sand
and found no condemnation.

I am woman in the crowd
who dared in faith to touch.
Such brief encounter
was my healing.

I, Mary of Magdala,
followed to the end,
weeping stood beside the tomb
and saw, I saw the risen Lord.

I, Lydia, seller of purple,
heard good news
and shared my baptism.

I am Tabitha,
finest of needleworkers,
raised from the dead.

Janet
Crawford
and
Erice
Webb

I am Mary.
I loved my baby
for which eternally I must wear
the patriarchal crown.
I beseech you, my sisters,
help me remove the weight
and lay it down.

28   **Broken silence**

O women whose voices have never been heard:
We repent of our deafness,
We confess our stubborn hearts and closed
        minds.

O women whose words have been consigned to
        silence:
We grieve for the wisdom which has been lost.

O women whose wisdom has not been heeded:
We desire that our time will be different and
We commit ourselves now to listen.
We will turn again to search out the scriptures.
We will look for the clues of your lives in the margins
        of history's pages.
We will seek out your words in secret places.
We will dig for your treasure hidden deep in the
        dark.

For we know our need of your wisdom.
We yearn for the restoration of what has been lost.
Our time is hungry for your forgotten stories,
Nicola For the ancient art of women's wisdom
Slee Which will heal our hurt and may yet save our world.

²⁹   **Wachet Auf**

Written on
Advent Sunday
1986, after
hearing the
Chorale Prelude
by Bach.

Advent.
Season when
Dual citizenship
Holds us in
Awkward tension.

The world, intent on
Spending Christmas,
Eats and drinks its way to
Oblivion after dinner.
The Kingdom sounds
Insistent warnings:
Repent, be ready,
Keep awake,
He comes.

Like some great fugue
The themes entwine:
The Christmas carols,
Demanding our attention
In shops and pubs,
Bore their insistent way
Through noise of traffic;
Underneath, almost unheard,
The steady solemn theme of
Advent.

With growing complexity,
Clashing, blending,
Rivals for our attention,
Themes mingle and separate,
Pulling us with increasing
Urgency,
Until in final resolution,
The end attained,
Harmony rests in aweful
Stillness, and
The child is born.

He comes,
Both Child and Judge.

Ann   And will he find us
Lewin   Watching?

30   **Merry Christmas**

At the heart of Christmas there was
Pain, bleeding and crying;
Love was with difficulty brought to birth.
Not to a sanitized stable did God come,
But to a world that needed mucking out;
His birth no tidy affair, but through
A single parent, in bed and breakfast
Shelter; an inconvenience, not welcomed
By bureaucrats with important business;
Acknowledged mainly by low-paid workers,
Foreign visitors, and animals.
The sequel: attempted murder, exile.

People wounded by indifference
Struggle to give love birth in the
Cold comfort of charity, largely
Unrecognized by those with power.
At the heart of Christmas, still there's
Pain, bleeding and crying,
A sword piercing the heart of God,
Opening the wounds of love.

Could we be midwives for the love of God,
Ann   Cradling that strength born in fragility,
Lewin   Delivering healing to a crying world?

³¹ **Of warriors and rebels**

They tell me Miriam means
beautiful rebel.
I like that.
Was always uneasy with
the unthinking 'holy' fiat;
passive 'doormat' imagery
of stereotypical femininity.

They tell me Gabriel means
avenging warrior,
a messenger whose 'Fear not'
shows God as master of biting irony.

They tell me the Magnificat
is a revolutionary song,
turning the world's ways upside down,
filling the starving with good things,
exalting the lowly.

Beautiful rebel, Miriam, Mary,
You fought against the desire
to run, to hide, to pretend you
hadn't heard the call to love and pain.

Warrior of God, avenging angel, Gabriel,
In paradox you spoke the truth.
In facing fear it disappears and frees the spirit,
as morning mist reveals the sun.

Beautiful rebel, Miriam, Mother,
You opened all to the God growing in you,
Body, mind and heart.
Nurture in us
a spirit of welcome and generosity.

Lady of liberation,
Forgive us   our conformity,
                 our sterility,

> our spiritual abortions
> and stillborn hopes.
>
> Foster in us
>   the spirit of revolution
>   that mirrors God's justice
> so that our souls too may glorify the Lord.

Mary
Hanrahan

32 Magnificat

> My heart is bubbling over with joy;
> with God it is good to be woman.
> From now on let all peoples proclaim:
> it is a wonderful gift to be.
> The one in whom power truly rests
> has lifted us up to praise;
> God's goodness shall fall like a shower
> on the trusting of every age.
> The disregarded have been raised up:
> the pompous and powerful shall fall.
> God has feasted the empty-bellied,
> and the rich have discovered their void.
> God has made good the word
> given at the dawn of time.

Phoebe
Willetts

33 The guest

> The pain being over
> now I feel the sense of loss.
> To see, to touch
> caress and kiss
> can never be the same
> as when my body
> was your home.
> Then you were mine
> and yet not mine.

For when you stirred
(although that was our secret)
I knew
the life contained within me
was not me.
You were my guest.
My body housed your need
until it grew too great.
And though
a little while
I can sustain you yet,
the first painful
parting's done;
from now
it is all partings.

From me you learn
to walk,
that you may be
the way that
I may learn to tread.

From me you learn
the words,
that you may speak
the truth
that I may comprehend.

From me you suck
the life,
that you may be
the living bread
that I may feed upon
and live.

From me you learn
the love
which is the sword
that pierces my heart through,
and nails you to the cross.

In your necessity
my dearest dear
you were the guest
I entertained.
Now you are the host
Rosemary   and at your table
Wakelin   I shall be sustained.

34   **We call them wise**

We call them wise
and I had always thought of them that way
respecting the pilgrimage of anyone
who sees a star and follows it
to his discomforting —
being prepared to change.
And yet —
in following their star, the star
that was to lead them to
enlargement of the soul (their own) —
they blundered mightily, and set in train
the massacre of many innocents.
Naive and foolish men they were, not wise,
to go and ask of Herod 'Where's
your rival, where
is he who might unseat you?'

I wonder if, back
in their own countries,
for all that they themselves were born again,
they heard the voice of Rachel
weeping for her children
Kate   refusing to be comforted
Compston   because they were no more?

³⁵   **In love revealed**

The busy crowd was thronging round;
A frightened woman, cursed for years,
Pushed through the throng and, trembling still,
Reached out and found you through her tears;
She touched your hem, and she was healed,
Behold, God's grace in love revealed.

The little girl was fading fast,
Her father dragged you to his door,
You banished those who wept and wailed,
She rose up, live and whole once more;
You kissed her cheek, and she was healed,
Behold, God's grace in love revealed.

They brought her to you to be stoned,
The woman caught in act of shame,
You turned their judgement into care,
And gave forgiveness, took her blame;
You touched her heart, and she was healed,
Behold, God's grace in love revealed.

The woman at the well was kind,
Though doubly outcast, did not shrink,
You told her of the spirit's need
For love more strong than food or drink;
You drank her cup, and she was healed,
Behold, God's grace in love revealed.

The woman of the streets broke in,
Where upright men made you their guest,
She poured her ointment on your feet,
You blessed her, laid her sins to rest;
She wiped your feet, and she was healed,
Behold, God's grace in love revealed.

The women, weeping, found the tomb,
Your body gone, the stone laid by,
You bade them tell the brothers how

Metre 88.88.88
(Many tunes
suitable, e.g.
Surrey, Sagina, St
Chrysostom)

Your love in death could never die;
They told the news, and all were healed,
Behold, God's grace in love revealed.

Through centuries of scorn and shame,
Your love has named us as your own,
Through poverty, despair and fear,
Our faith and hopefulness have grown;
You touch us, and we all are healed,
Behold, God's grace in love revealed.

Anna
Briggs

36 **Who touched me?**

Prepared at the
first Methodist
Consultation for
Women
Ministers,
Charney Manor,
Oxford,
September 1984.

(Mark 5.24–34)

We all bleed.
We bleed for ourselves — we each
have our private pain.
We bleed for others;
and we bleed for a wounded world.
If we did not bleed for others at some
times and in some measure,
would we not be spiritually barren?
Unfit for our calling.
Incapable of conceiving and nurturing new life,
in forming relationships and caring communities.
But if the pain takes over,
the bleeding becomes constant.
Do we not then find that we have
lost touch with our Lord —
He is obscured by the crowd of our
concerns — the crowd of our activities —
perhaps even the crowd of our own words.
Jesus, help us to touch you now,
to lay before you our own, and the world's pain.
Help us as we wait in silence
to feel your hands upon us.

37 **Living water**

On dry, relentless paths
through stone and sand
of a thirsty land,
a man has come
to Jacob's well,
empty-handed.
And a woman is here
clasping in her hands
a jar of precious water.
Her care is that there should be
no spill, no waste,
no dripping away.
As the man speaks
of ordinary needs
and extraordinary relationships,
an outrageous splash
of pure ecstasy
gives life
to the meeting.
Living water runs free,
sweeping along hearts
grown hard as stone;
washing dusty feet
and unready hands.
This water is a precious promise
of new life
for tired people;
a flowing, moving joy,
seeking to quench human thirst
and ease everlasting sorrows.
This water is that truth
which like music or love
flows out of us
continually,
and takes us to the edge
of the abyss

Joy of faith, without the safety
Mead of a bucket or water jar.

38   The prayer Jesus taught us

'Widening the
Web', Indigo
Gate, Greenham
Common,
December 1985.

God, lover of us all, most holy one,
help us to respond to you
to create what you want for us here on earth.
Give us today enough for our needs;
forgive our weak and deliberate offences,
just as we must forgive others
when they hurt us.
Help us to resist evil
and to do what is good;
for we are yours,

Lala
Winkley

endowed with your power
to make our world whole.

39   Andrewtide

(In John's Gospel
it was Andrew
who brought the
boy with the
loaves and fishes
to Jesus. In John
this is also the
'institution
narrative'.)

The crowd had listened to your word,
With love their hearts and minds were fired,
The miracle of what they heard
Still kept them close, though hungry, tired.

As daylight left the crowded slope,
You saw their simple, human need,
Sent Andrew and the rest in hope,
To find, to gather, and to feed.

The smallest gift a child could share,
Some bread, two fishes, simple food,
Broke in your hands to love and care,
To feed the hungry multitude.

Like Andrew, now we turn and seek;
Earth's hunger haunts us, stark and real;
We fear the gifts we find too weak
The world's distress to touch and heal.

Tune: Angelus, or
any other slow,
reflective 8.8.8.8.
tune.

Now send us, searching, for the gift
That hides in every human soul,
That in your hands sin's power can shift
And make your world and people whole.

Use us, your friends, to seek and trace
The gift that seems of smallest worth,
To shape the miracle of grace,
The love to feed a hungry earth.

*Anna
Briggs*

40   Just a housewife

I packed five cakes of bread and two small fishes,
Sent him off, my youngest lad,
To take his father's dinner to the field.

Came back alone he did, all goggle-eyed.

My fresh-baked bread that varmint gave away
To some young travelling preacher out of Galilee.
It fed five thousand people. What a tale!

It can't be true . . . but if it is . . .
What kind of dough did these hands knead
This morning?

*Cordelia
Baker-Pearce*

41   In the house of Simon the Leper

From a sermon on
Mark 14.3–9
(1982).

Imagine yourself in the house of Simon, the leper. You
find yourself at table with Jesus and with others, when
all of a sudden your dinner conversation is interrupted
by a woman who comes, not to serve at table as might
be appropriate, but to take Jesus' attention away from
you and to focus all attention on herself. The room
gradually falls silent, all conversation ceases and you
wait, both curious and affronted, to see what is going
to happen.

The woman comes to Jesus at the table. She walks silently, seeming not to notice you all sitting there. She carries a small alabaster jar and when she reaches Jesus she breaks the seal and pours the ointment inside the jar over his head. Jesus stays still; he neither welcomes nor rejects the woman, but he allows her to anoint him and he recognizes the significance of what she is doing to him: in anointing him she is preparing him for burial. And Jesus feels the fear of his own impending death, the aloneness of his own life, and it is as if he and the woman alone understand what this means. There are no words, only your own bewilderment at what your eyes are seeing and the sweet-smelling fragrance of the ointment gradually filling the room and your senses.

The silence begins to fill with mutterings, indignant and even angry. What the hell is this woman doing? Doesn't she know how much that ointment costs? Just think what else we could have bought for the poor with that sum! What a waste! And he just sits there letting her do it — I thought he wasn't meant to be into hero-worship or this kind of extravagant pantomime. And who does she think she is anyway? And Simon, the host, the leper, stays silent. He is one of the sick, one of the poor who is always with you, and he understands that the money is nothing and that the anointing is everything. The woman without a name has done something that only she can do and which cannot be logically or rationally justified, but which breaks a silence. She shows to you at the table that your moral package deal can be turned on its head. She has told you how it is, not as you think it ought to be; she tells you that this man Jesus will die. And what good has it done anyway? Economically, it has been a loss; for a meal-time the woman has been an intrusion. But for Jesus and for the woman and maybe for Simon too 'she has done what is in her power to do'. And perhaps when you see Jesus crucified or hear of his death, you will remember this house, this meal, this
Elaine woman and you will too understand the need to break
Willis the silence.

From 'Beforehand
for the Burial',
Women In
Theology
quiet day, Holy
Week, 1985.

42   **Women anointing Jesus**

God our Love-Maker,

We are afraid of your love, your intimacy.
We are used to being judged,
but we are not used to being loved, totally.
We would rather hold on to our self-hatred
than believe in your total acceptance of us.

Give us the courage to let go and embrace you;
may we learn how to want you to touch us, to know
        us,
that we in our turn may love generously
those who cannot believe they are loved.
Amen.
(Luke 7.36–50)

God our Pain-Bearer,

Give us the courage of this unknown woman,
to speak the gospel with authority
from the place of no authority;
to break open all our resources
from the place of no resources;
to break open and pour out
even the pain that we want to hold on to;
so that we can dare to name the truth about our world,
and truthfully stand with the one
who made himself nothing for our sake,
Jesus Christ, our Lord.
Amen.
(Mark 14.3–11)

God our Life-Giver,

Again and again we find ourselves stuck
in old patterns of domination and submission;
we stay resenting our powerlessness
or guilt-ridden by our power.

Give us courage to believe that change is possible:
let us so wash one another's feet as friends
that the fragrance of our ministry
may fill the whole church;
and free us with the symbol of slavery
to make a world where no one is in bondage.
In the name of the one who died to give us life,
Jesus Christ.

Janet   Amen.
Morley   (John 12.1–8)

43 **Letter from Pilate's wife to her sister in Rome**

My dear Claudia

Many thanks for your last letter; I'm glad the family
remains well, and congratulations to Marcus – I bet he
looks frightfully grand in his purple! He's obviously
managing to keep on the right side of You-Know-Who
– long may it continue!

It's still grim here – and getting more fraught by
the minute. It's always been a notorious black spot of
course – it's *incredibly* volatile.

Trust Pontius to get landed with it – it makes
me sick! I *told* him we were better off where we
were, without the promotion, where he had Flavius
to advise him – but no, he took no notice as usual –
fussed on about upsetting Sejanus if he turned it
down.

I said, 'What about upsetting *me*?' to which he
replied that he didn't think me capable of performing
what Sejanus had done to his half-brother Gaius who'd
refused to go to Cilicia; and *that's* true enough.

So here we are, staving off daily riots by the skin
of our teeth, with no support at all from Pompeius
Flaccus in Syria (do you remember his sister Lesbia?
She was married to Marcellus eventually – they've
ended up in *Caledonia*!)

Flaccus wants Sejanus out, I think – heaven knows what would happen to Pontius if he should succeed; that patronage is all that stands between him and kingdom come at present.

He's really out of his depth here – *anyone* would be! The things they get worked up about – you wouldn't believe it!

Mainly the priestly caste (as usual!). It's virtually a theocracy here, you know! They've only *got* one god – a sort of combination of Jupiter and Mars. The temple to him is in the middle of the city – massive affair – gold roof – the lot – they take it all *terribly seriously*. It's instant *death* for any dissident who might raise his head with an alternative version! (Lucius would have a *fit* if he could see it after being in Greece for three years!)

And we're not short of the usual crop of young gallants offering to free their country from 'The Yoke of *Rome*' – but *these* are sort of religious *as well*.

There was one the other day that I got really upset about; he was doing *good magic* around the place – you know the sort of thing – and got on the wrong side of the priests who couldn't work out how he did it; at least that's what Julia told me.

They got hold of him and sentenced him to *death* in one of those kangaroo courts, and Pontius had to sort it out the next day.

The night before I had the weirdest dream about this young chap; I dreamt that no one had any eyes – all those blank, eyeless faces – really scary – no one except him, and individuals in his vicinity, who then grew eyes out of their own. Zombie-like priests dragged him off, and Pontius, eyeless like all the rest, let them *lynch* him.

I woke up gasping and sweating – it was so real, Claudia; I've never had a dream like it.

Pontius was already in court when I woke up, so I sent Julia over with a note to tell him to leave this young chap alone; it really *was* good magic he was practising – but that malevolent little faction threatened to incite riots and he just washed his hands of the whole thing. Really feeble he was, and the young sorcerer ended up on Hangman's Hill – it was totally *foul*, Claudia.

All Pontius did when he got home was to heave a sigh of relief that a riot hadn't happened; it's the worst time of year for them at the moment – one of their big festivals. Julia says it's to celebrate their god's parting the seas or something. And they really *believe* it!

Anyway, we've got through the latest crisis for the moment –

Burn some incense for me, Claudia.
With all good wishes to you and the family,

Your affectionate sister,

Win
English   Livia

44   **Fifteen years later: Jairus's daughter in conversation with her friend Sarah**

I don't know about you, Sarah, but I wouldn't want my childhood over again. Not my early teens, anyway. I think it was the worst time of my life. I was so terrified of everything, mainly of growing up, really. But nobody would listen to my fears. There were so many things I wanted to ask my mother about, but she was always too busy, or didn't seem to want to answer my questions. I realize now that she probably didn't know the answers herself.

My father was always kind but mostly away in the synagogue; and in any case, they were not questions I could ask a man. My brother Joshua was two years older than me and everyone thought he was wonderful, especially my mother and father. I loved him too and we played together a lot. He was very clever and could read the scriptures at a very early age. I wanted to read them too but my father said that it was not necessary for a girl to be able to read.

As he got older Josh didn't want to play with me any more and spent a lot of time in the synagogue with my father. I had to help my mother do the cooking and serve my brother at table. We had servants but my mother always prepared the food. I became good at cooking; it was the one thing I did that received some notice and some praise.

But gradually, I found I didn't want to eat any of it. I pretended to eat it of course, and nobody noticed for a long time that I had become very thin. I had no energy left and I knew in my heart of hearts that I didn't really want to go on living.

Eventually my family realized what was happening and tried to coax me to eat. But I just couldn't, not even to please my father. The thought of becoming a woman was unbearable to me; all that blood and uncleanness and being banished to the women's quarter every month. I couldn't face it and I think my soul made the decision to depart from this life.

And then one day – I had been lying on my bed for over a month and I really felt as if I had died.

I was floating above my bed and saw myself lying there deathly white and still and I saw everyone crying. My mother was in despair, rocking back and forth in her chair beside the bed.

But then I heard a voice call my name. It was as if my body were calling me back very urgently and I had to obey it. Then I became aware of a rabbi sitting near me. He had a kind voice. He held my hand and talked to me for a long time about how lovely it was to be a grown woman and that I had nothing to fear from bleeding every month; that it was a sign of a healthy womb, capable of bearing children, if I wanted them; that there was nothing unclean about womankind,

that God loved me and everything about me. Sarah,
he seemed to know, and answer, all those
unanswered questions that had filled me with fear
for so long!

And then he said something amazing; he said that
I must love my body and everything about it, including
my menstrual blood, because it is full of God. He said I
am made of God-stuff, that we all are, and everything
in the whole universe – and that's why we must look
after ourselves and the world, because they are beautiful
and sacred and full of God. And he said that's why I
must decide to get better, so that I could sing and
dance and enjoy life to the full.

And do you know Sarah, I knew at that moment
that that was what I wanted to do. I sat up in bed and
said 'I'm hungry!' and the rabbi laughed and asked my
mother to bring me something to eat. He looked so
beautiful when he laughed that I just gazed and gazed
at him. I knew at that moment that I would love
him all the days of my life. His name was Jesus of
Nazareth.

You can imagine the effect of all this on my
family. Their joy and their love for this man who had
brought me back to them was overwhelming and we
Joan begged him to make his home with us. But he said that
E. James he could not; that he had far to go and not much time.

⁴⁵ **The way of the cross**

This piece is
intended for 8–16
women's voices:
3–5 women
hanging ('hingin')
out of their
windows
watching the

(Luke 23.28)

Daughters of Jerusalem, do not weep for me,
but weep for yourselves and for your children.

Daughters, do not weep for me
Weep for yourselves
Weep for your children

passers by, 1 or 2 prostitutes, a drug addict, a glue sniffer, a woman struggling with a pram, 1 or 2 women loaded down with shopping, a homeless woman begging, etc. It was originally performed by the Church Women's Resource Group based in Glasgow.

Jesus saw the city and wept over it

Weep woman
Weak woman
Weep

As Jesus wept
Weep woman
Unclean woman
Unfit to serve
Unfit to celebrate

The woman touched him and was healed
He touched
He was touched
He broke the taboo
Who has reinstated it?
Weep woman
Be silent and weep
Second class citizen
Say nothing

Tell them I have risen
Speak woman
Tell them I have risen
Weep woman
Submit, obey
Chattel
You have nothing to say

And she said nothing
But anointed the Christ, the Messiah, the anointed one of God
She knew
But said nothing
And did what she could
Weep woman
Work woman
Fetch and carry
And do not complain
Would you mind giving me a hand with the pram?
Stand up woman
Be straight
You are set free

Weep woman
Weep for your children
Who have no home
 We must lock up the church
 People will mess it up
 Tramps might sleep in it
 Our valuable ornaments could be stolen
  Whoever welcomes one such child in my
   name welcomes me
  Whoever welcomes me welcomes the one
   who sent me
Weep woman
Weep for your children
Weep for those whose lives are wasted
 Let them work
  There is no work
  Have you got ten pence for a cup of tea?
 Let them wait and queue
 Lend them money
 Keep them in debt
 Make them grateful
 Make them repay
  From what?
 Poverty must be paid for
 Our taxes will rise
 We cannot have that
  Whatever you do to the least of these you do
   to me
Weep woman
Weep for your children
Weep for those who are used and abused
Weep for the child who learns to pay with her body
Weep for the child who learns to sell her body
  Are you looking for business?
  Who has done this?
   It would be better for you if a great
   millstone were hung round your neck
 It doesn't happen here
 Not in my street

Not in my life
> Open your eyes
> Open your ears
> It happens here
> Listen to the children
>> Unless you become like little children

Linda Daughters of Jerusalem, do not weep for me, weep for
Hill yourselves and for your children.

46 **The women**

Powerless to effect a rescue.
Not for us
The melodramatic gestures of the men.
If we had swords, would we have acted thus?
No: mutilation's not our kind of game.
But, unlike men, we didn't turn and flee;
We followed at a distance, doggedly,
Mocked by the soldiers, jostled by the crowd . . .
And we were there
To hear that cry that sounded like despair.
We shared her pain
When she held his body in her arms again,
And took her home, and kissed her poor wan face,
Rocked her to sleep at last in our embrace
And waited all the night
And all the Sabbath for the first sad light
Of the ensuing day.
And then, with spices, we were on our way:
Burial and birth we know.
But, as we neared
The place, mist cleared:
We saw the stone rolled back
And hesitated by the yawning black
Mouth, then we went in,
Groping to find only an empty shroud.

Suddenly, there was light; warmth glowed.
We left the cave reborn
And ran home, laughing aloud.

But one stayed behind,
Magdalene. Was it tears that made her blind?
She told us later that she had to stay
Close to the place where her beloved lay.
So she was first to meet him,
To undo the traitor's kiss and greet him.
We thought it right
She should be chosen for delight.
But, when she told the men,
Incredulous, as of us, they jeered and then
Ran off to see for themselves. The rest is told.

Joan But just remember: men recount the story,
Smith We women were the first to see the glory.

47 **Stations of the cross: Mary meets Jesus**

How can I bear it?
I see you, my son,
staggering, weighed down
by the cruel burden of the cross
and the jeering of the crowd.

Before the world ever saw you,
it was I who carried you,
growing like a secret seed,
dancing in the darkness of the womb.
It was I who sang to you,
telling out the greatness of God,
though people scorned my singleness
in the littleness of their lives.
Because I said yes to God,
I had to be strong for my child:
you were the burden that I bore with love.

You were the baby that I bore with pain
in the crowded stable,
in the obscure darkness,
among the creatures, their sound and smell.
Your first cry was where my humanity
stretched to the limit, was healed,
with the joy of new life,
while God laughed.

Like any new-born child,
you were small, needy, fragile.
We had our work cut out
to keep you safe, in a hard world
between the swords of Herod's soldiers
and the splinters in Joseph's workshop.

How could I bear it
when you grew up and, among your friends,
used hard words to put me in my place:
saying 'Whoever does the will
of my heavenly Father
is my mother, my brother'?

You had no time
for false sentiment about mothers:
you had other work to do.
But I was the one who,
before you were born,
said 'I am the Lord's servant –
so be it.'
In my body, God's word
was transformed into flesh.
So, as you turned water into wine,
and fed crowds with bread,
I had courage to bear your hard words
because I too had a part in God's work
and could bear witness to hope.

But what transformation can happen now?
We are both trapped
in what happens daily to ordinary people
who see no end to their suffering —
while God weeps.
We are both being torn apart
because, in the weight of that cross,
you are bearing the sins of the whole world.

I want to hide my eyes.
But I step from the crowd,
and reach out my hand
to offer my love, my strength, my pain.
God knows how I can bear it.

*Jan
Sutch
Pickard*

48   Pieta

This was written
as a companion
poem to 'The
guest' (p. 37).

Your work accomplished,
now I know the sharpness of the sword
that pierces my heart through.
Again I hold you in my arms,
caress and kiss
that dearest form
which carried all my love.
But as I watched you grow
I knew
the life in you I nurtured
had a purpose I found hard to bear —
for you were mine and yet not mine,
for, though you loved me
as my dearest son,
I knew your being drew
its inner life
from the mysterious One
you called your Father:
and as you taught and healed
and blessed,
his love in you
embraced all humankind.

I touch your wounded feet
which walked the way
that led you to the cross.

I kiss your silent lips
which spoke the truth
the powerful still reject.

I feel the stillness
of your lifeless heart and know
the light of life itself has died.

The piercing grief
and weight of total loss
are now commensurate
with the joy I knew
in this my dearest love.

Now others wrap you round
and lay you
in your waiting tomb —

And waiting
night and day
and night
until I feel the stirring
in that earthy womb,
and pain and grief
and loss and death,
which laboured in you
for your victory
give birth
to Life and Truth,
Your living Way,
Rosemary   and break out in the glory
Wakelin   of your Easter day.

49   New birth – a midrash

For a long time I kept silent; I did not answer my people.
But now the time to act has come; I cry out like a woman
in labour. Do not think that I will bring my people to the
point of birth and not let them be born. Rejoice with
Jerusalem and be glad for her. (Isaiah 42.14; 66.9)

They were there, of course, the midwives
reluctant witnesses to the agony of the labouring
          woman.
They stayed,
honour-bound by their calling,
to the bitter end.

But today, for once, they were helpless;
their skills and knowledge were to no avail
in the face of inevitable death.
All they could offer her
was the comfort of their presence
and the warmth of their love.

As the agony of labour dragged on
they talked in low voices
of the child
to whom the mother battled to give birth.
'It is so premature,
how can it possibly survive?'
said Mary.
Joanna agreed –
'If ever a child needed its mother, this one does.'

They wept for their dying friend
for shared memories
for lost opportunities
for the futility of it all.

They wept for the child
so soon to be orphaned.

Then, finally,
with one last shuddering, anguished
push
the child was born
through the flesh, cruelly torn apart:
a child,
perfectly formed,
and breathing with the miracle of new life.

'It is finished' sighed the mother
and died.

Her friends, the midwives,
wailing,
unable to hold back their grief
tended to the broken body,
their ministrations too soon interrupted
by the child's first cries.

'What a lusty cry for one so fragile'
said Mary, smiling through her tears,
cradling the precious new life.

'We will nourish you and protect you.
We will give you our strength,
we will not allow your precious life
to flicker out.

Alison In our care you will flourish
Horvat and in you, your mother will live again.'

50   **'Woman, why are you weeping?'**

(A dramatic reading for many voices)

Jesus said, 'Woman, why are you weeping?'
'I weep because I am old and no one takes any notice
of old women.'

Anna was eighty-four years old and still serving in the Temple when she recognized and proclaimed the infant Jesus as the promised Holy One of Israel.

It is good news for old women today when the church recognizes and draws on their wisdom and experience.

Jesus said, 'Woman, why are you weeping?'
'I weep because I am a single mother struggling to feed and clothe my children.'

Jesus saw the distress of the widow who had lost her son, had compassion on her, and restored him to life.

It is good news for women today when the church supports them in their struggles to bring up their children.

Jesus said, 'Woman, why are you weeping?'
'I weep because when I and other women explore the Bible and do theology together our work is not taken seriously.'

Mary sat at Jesus' feet and listened as he taught, and the Samaritan woman debated with him about God.

It is good news for women today when the church recognizes the authenticity of feminist theology.

Jesus said, 'Woman, why are you weeping?'
'I weep because I bleed when I should not, and there is no healing.'

The woman with the haemorrhage had been bleeding for twelve years and when she touched the hem of Jesus' garment she was cured.

It is good news for women today when the church takes seriously issues of women's health.

Jesus said, 'Woman, why are you weeping?'
'I weep because I am living with a man to whom I'm not married, and the church refuses to accept my ministry.'

Jesus knew that the Samaritan woman had had five husbands and was living in a *de facto* relationship, and yet continued to talk with her as an equal.

It is good news for women today when the church accepts their sexuality, and does not condemn their relationships.

Jesus said, 'Woman, why are you weeping?'
'I weep because I'm bowed down so my eyes are fastened on the ground. I cannot raise my head.'

Jesus called the crippled woman to him, laid hands on her, and immediately she stood up straight.

It is good news for women today when the church empowers them to stand tall in the community.

Jesus said, 'Woman, why are you weeping?'
'I weep because I'm on drugs, I sell my body on the streets, and I am an outcast.'

Jesus ate with prostitutes and sinners, and scandalized the smugly respectable by accepting the intimate touch of a woman who was a notorious sinner.

It is good news for women today when the church embraces the outcasts, and works against all forms of sexual exploitation.

Jesus said, 'Woman, why are you weeping?'
'I weep because I have no children and am tired of questions and pitying comments.'

Jesus said that blessing comes to those who hear the
word of God and obey it.

**It is good news for women today when the church
frees them from the expectation that true fulfilment
comes from having children.**

*Janet
Crawford
and
Erice
Fairbrother*

**Good news is
freedom
healing, support
affirmation, empowerment
forgiveness, acceptance
love.**

⁵¹ **1 Corinthians 12.31—13.1–13: Beatrice Version**

A re-working of
this passage into
the language and
feel' of 1992 for
the funeral of
Dominic Seddon
(5.01.64 –
2.06.92) by his
sister.

Be ambitious, reach out for the higher gifts. And I
am going to show you a way that is the best of them
all:

If I had the eloquence of poets or of angels, but spoke
without love, I'd be an untuned instrument, or a cracked
    voice.
If I had the gift of prophecy, understanding all the
mysteries of this.world, and knowing everything, if I
had the greatest faith, to move mountains or to cure
ills, but without love I'd be worthless.
If I gave away all that I possessed, piece by piece, and
if I even let them take my body to do what they
would, if there was no love, I'd be nothing.

Love is always patient and kind; it is never jealous;
love is never arrogant or conceited; it is never rude or
    selfish;
it doesn't take offence, and is not resentful.

Love does not dwell in aversion, but rejoices in the
  truth;
it is always ready to forgive, to trust, and to endure
  whatever comes.

Love does not come to an end. But if there are
prophecies, they only apply to a finite time; the time
will come when they can tell us no more. If there are
words, they cannot give us language for ever. And
knowledge – even for this, the time will come when it
is lost and of no importance. For our knowledge is
imperfect, and our prophesying is imperfect; but once
perfection comes, all imperfect things will disappear, all
the bad will be gone.

When I was a child, I used to talk like a child, and think
like a child, and argue like a child. But now I am full
grown and all childish things are put behind me. Where
as a child I saw it with clarity, now it is not so clear –
a dim reflection in a mirror. What I know now is
incomplete, but when the time comes, I shall understand
all things, and we shall be seeing each other face to
face.

In other words, there are three things that are really
worth while – faith, and hope, and love; and of these
Beatrice highest of gifts the most special, the most important,
Seddon the one we all need, is love.

52   Let us now praise noble women

Let us now praise noble women
    and our mothers who lived before us,
Through whom God's glory has been shown,
    in each successive generation.
Some ruled nations with authority
    and were renowned as queens;
others gave counsel by their wisdom

and spoke with prophetic power;
a few were leaders of the people
    because of their deep understanding;
    their custody of tradition.
Some composed musical tunes
    and set forth verses in writing;
others were rich and respected
    peacefully keeping their homes.
All these were honoured in their lifetime
    and were a glory of their day.
Such women have left a name which is remembered
    so that their praises are still sung.
But others have left no memory,
    have vanished as though they had never lived.
These are the nameless women of the ages;
    the work of their hands is not remembered.
These women planted, picked,
    preserved, baked, boiled and brewed;
they washed, cooked, cleaned,
    fed, clothed and nursed the world.
A few were barren but most bore
    children, children and more children
To carry on the father's name
    so his posterity continues forever.
All these were different in their lives,
    different and yet the same;
and they died in different ways,
    in childbirth, sickness,
fever, madness, ripe old age;
    all died.
They are now as though they had never been
    and so too are their daughters who followed them.
There are numerous men whose good works have not
      been forgotten
    whose descendants remember their names
    and recall their forefathers with pride,
    rejoicing in their heritage.
Their bodies were buried with honour
    and their names live on
    so that their glory lasts for ever.

Few of our foremothers are so remembered;
  most lie forgotten in their graves
until their daughters shall claim their inheritance,
  recollecting them with joy and pride.
Now their glory is not blotted out
    as we declare their wisdom and proclaim their
      praise;

Janet Noble women and nameless ones,
Crawford   our mothers who lived before us.

53 **Collects**

God, our sustainer,
You have called out your people into the wilderness
to travel your unknown ways.
Make us strong to leave behind false security and
    comfort,
and give us new hope in our calling;
that the desert may blossom as a rose,
and your promises may be fulfilled in us.
In the name of Jesus Christ. **Amen.**

54 O God, the power of the powerless,
you have chosen as your witnesses
those whose voice is not heard.
Grant that, as women first announced the resurrection
though they were not believed,
we too may have courage
to persist in proclaiming your word,
in the power of Jesus Christ. **Amen.**

55 O God, our beloved,
born of a woman's body;
you came that we might look upon you,
and handle you with our own hands.
Grant that we may so cherish one another in our
    bodies

that we may also be touched by you,
through the Word made flesh,
Jesus Christ. **Amen**.

56   God our Mother,
you hold our life within you,
nourish us at your breast,
and teach us to walk alone.
Help us so to receive your tenderness
and respond to your challenge
that others may draw life from us,
in your name. **Amen**.

57   O God our deliverer,
you cast down the mighty,
and lift up those of no account;
as Elizabeth and Mary embraced
with songs of liberation,
so may we also be pregnant with your Spirit,
and affirm one another in hope for the world,
through Jesus Christ. **Amen**.

58   O God, our soul's desire,
whose integrity is beyond our imagining,
and whose loveliness is more than we can bear,
make our hearts restless to seek your truth
in every part of our life;
that we may look upon your beauty without fear,
and find our rest in you,
through Jesus Christ. **Amen**.

59   O God whose Word is life,
and whose delight is to answer our cry,
give us faith like the Syro-Phoenician woman,
who refused to remain an outsider;
that we too may have the wit to argue
and demand that our daughters be made whole,
through Jesus Christ. **Amen**.

60 O covenant God,
    You call us to the risk of commitment
    even from the place of despair.
    As Ruth and Naomi loved and held to one another,
    abandoning the ways of the past;
    so may we also not be divided,
    but travel together
    into that strange land where you will lead us,
    through Jesus Christ. **Amen.**

61 God our creator,
    You have made us one with this earth,
    to tend it and to bring forth fruit;
    may we so respect and cherish
    all that has life from you,
    that we may share in the labour of all creation
    to give birth to your hidden glory.
    through Jesus Christ. **Amen.**

62 O God, in whose weakness is our strength,
    you have taught us not to trust in armed might,
    nor in the weapons of war.
    As Jesus also suffered outside the gate,
    let us go forth with him;
    that the gates of hell may not prevail against us,

Janet   and that we may embrace even our enemies,
Morley   through Jesus Christ our saviour. **Amen.**

63 **New collects**

    God whose holy name
    defies our definition,
    but whose will is known
    in freeing the oppressed:
    make us to be one
    with all who cry for justice;
    that we who speak your praise
    may struggle for your truth,
    through Jesus Christ. **Amen.**

64   O God,
        you have made us for yourself,
        and against your longing there is no defence.
        Mark us with your love,
        and release in us a passion for your justice
        in our disfigured world;
        that we may turn from our guilt and face you,
        our heart's desire. **Amen.**

65   O God, the source of all insight,
        whose coming was revealed to the nations
        not among men of power
        but on a woman's lap:
        give us grace to seek you
        where you may be found,
        that the wisdom of this world may be humbled
        and discover your unexpected joy,
        through Jesus Christ. **Amen.**

66   Christ, whose bitter agony
        was watched from afar by women:
        enable us to follow the example
        of their persistent love;
        that, being steadfast in the face of horror,
        we may also know the place of resurrection,
        in your name. **Amen.**

67   God of terror and joy,
        you arise to shake the earth.
        Open our graves
        and give us back the past;
        so that all that has been buried
        may be freed and forgiven,
        and our lives may return to you
        through the risen Christ. **Amen.**

68   O God for whom we long
        as a woman in labour
        longs for her delivery:
        give us courage to wait,

strength to push,
and discernment to know the right time;
that we may bring into the world
your joyful peace,
through Jesus Christ. **Amen.**

69   Spirit of truth
whom the world can never grasp,
touch our hearts
with the shock of your coming;
fill us with desire
for your disturbing peace;
and fire us with longing
to speak your uncontainable word
through Jesus Christ. **Amen.**

70   God of truth and terror,
whose word we can with comfort
neither speak nor contain;
give us courage to release the fire
you have shut up in our bones,
and strength in your spirit
Janet   to withstand the burning,
Morley   through Jesus Christ. **Amen.**

⁷¹ **Bone of my bone**

*Then the eyes of both were opened, and they knew that they
were naked; and they . . . hid themselves from the presence
of the Lord God.
(Genesis 3.7, 8 RSV)*

Loving Creator, we confess that as women and men
we have distorted your image in us.
We confess our misuse of power;
we have sought to dominate others, and to impose our
    will by force or threat;
we have learned to manipulate and deceive, and feared
    to confront injustice.

We repent before God, and before our sisters and
    brothers.

Men: **You are bone of my bone**
Women: **And flesh of my flesh.**

We confess our misuse of our faculties:
we have prevented ourselves from feeling compassion
    and tenderness;
we have failed in courage and understanding, and
    denied the gifts we have.

We repent before God, and before our sisters and
    brothers.

Men: **You are bone of my bone**
Women: **And flesh of my flesh.**

We confess our misuse of sexuality:
we have found pleasure in the degrading of others'
    bodies;
we have failed to respect and care for our own bodies;
we have chosen to condemn, rather than to delight in
    each other.

We repent before God, and before our sisters and
    brothers.

Men: **You are bone of my bone**
Women: **And flesh of my flesh.**

We confess that we have failed to obey God first:
we have made an idol of our work, our status, and our
    possessions;
we have sought all our meaning in another human
    being;
we have made a society based on aggression and fear,
where love is a private luxury.

We repent before God, and before our sisters and
    brothers.

Men: **You are bone of my bone**
Women: **And flesh of my flesh.**

We confess that we have created a world where,
    between women and men,
there is violence and fear, resentment and distrust.
We seek God's forgiveness and reconciling love,
that we may learn to do justice,
and so come without shame
before the one who delights in the human race.

We affirm before God, and before our sisters and
    brothers.

Janet   *Men:*   **You are bone of my bone**
Morley *Women:*   **And flesh of my flesh.**

72   **The sharing**

We told our stories —
That's all.
We sat and listened to
Each other
And heard the journeys
Of each soul.
We sat in silence
Entering each one's pain and
Sharing each one's joy.
We heard love's longing
And the lonely reachings-out
For love and affirmation.
We heard of dreams
Shattered.
And visions fled.
Of hopes and laughter
Turned stale and dark.
We felt the pain of
Isolation and
The bitterness
Of death.

But in each brave and
Lonely story
God's gentle life
Broke through
And we heard music in
The darkness
And smelt flowers in
The void.

We felt the budding
Of creation
In the searchings of
Each soul
And discerned the beauty
Of God's hand in
Each muddy, twisted path.

And his voice sang
In each story
His life sprang from
Each death.
Our sharing became
One story
Of a simple lonely search
For life and hope and
Oneness
In a world which sobs
For love.
And we knew that in
Our sharing
God's voice with
Mighty breath
Was saying
Love each other and
Take each other's hand.

For you are one
Though many
And in each of you
I live.
So listen to my story
And share my pain
And death.
Oh, listen to my story
Edwina   And rise and live
Gateley   With me.

₇₃ **Lent**

Do not retreat into your private world,
That place of safety, sheltered from the storm,
Where you may tend your garden, seek your soul,
And rest with loved ones where the fire burns warm.

To tend a garden is a precious thing,
But dearer still the one where all may roam,
The weeds of poison, poverty and war,
Demand your care, who call the earth your home.

To seek your soul it is a precious thing,
But you will never find it on your own,
Only among the clamour, threat and pain
Of other people's need will love be known.

To rest with loved ones is a precious thing,
But peace of mind exacts a higher cost,
Your children will not rest and play in quiet,
While they still hear the crying of the lost.

Do not retreat into your private world,
There are more ways than firesides to keep warm;
Kathy   There is no shelter from the rage of life,
Galloway So meet its eye, and dance within the storm.

74   **Acceptable losses?**

The men on the screen
Use language that cleans up war;
Talk of surgical precision
Taking out enemy power,
Leave unseen the effects
Of the not-so-smart weapons:
The homes being bombed,
The fear and the deaths and the maiming.
They assure us, unwilling voyeurs,
That our side is performing to plan.
Ours? Who asked us to join?
We are caught, like the cormorants
Ann   Oiled with our evil,
Lewin Reluctant participants in war.

⁷⁵ **Re-igniting fires of justice**

Excerpt from a
liturgy intended
to challenge all
people to work
against racism, to
be used 'for any
time people need
to be reminded
and supported to
do the work of
justice'.

Community Response

Weep, O my sisters and brothers,
Weep for innocent ones massacred;
Weep for those who are homeless;
Weep for those who are unemployed;
Weep for those who survive violence;
Weep for daughters and sons captured,
     tortured, and disappeared;
Weep for mothers humbled and enslaved;
Weep for fathers killed;
Weep for . . . . (*name what you weep for*)
Weep, O my sisters and brothers,
Weep until wisdom arises
     from fires of justice.
Amen. Blessed Be. Let It Be So.

Ritual of Ashes: Blessing of Ashes

(Four blessers each pick up a bowl of ashes, and say in turn)

1. Blessed are you, Holy One, Searing Fire, for reminding us that we must fast from racism in all of its forms.
2. Blessed are you, Holy One, Shedder of Tears, for calling us to weep for injustice done to innocent people.
3. Blessed are you, Holy One, Sorrowful Mother, for giving us these ashes as a symbol of our mourning.
4. Blessed are you, Holy One, Future Hope, for urging us to re-ignite fires of Justice.

Rite of Sharing Ashes

The four blessers anoint one another's hands and forehead with ashes, responding with 'we rise again from ashes'. They then put ashes on the participants.

Ritual of Healing

We wear these ashes as a sign that brokenness, fragmentation, and disintegration exist within our world, within our country, within our cities, within us. We carry the ashes of ourselves and of those who have gone before us. Look round the room. Notice the ashes. Remember the evil in our society.

We must bring our life out of these ashes. Therefore, we not only put on ashes, but we also wash them away as a sign that we gather our wisdom together to overcome racism in all its forms. If you would like to, invite one of the blessers to wash off your ashes and give you a candle. Respond with: 'I will bring new life out of these ashes. I will re-ignite fires of justice.' Light a candle and place it anywhere . . .

Sending Forth

Let us rise again from ashes,
> from anger that we have felt,
> from dreams we have not fully dreamed.
>> Let us re-ignite fires of justice.
Response: **Let us re-ignite fires of justice.**

Let us rise again from ashes,
> from the good that we have not done,
> from the pain and suffering we have known.
>> Let us re-ignite fires of justice.
Response: **Let us re-ignite fires of justice.**

Let us rise again from ashes,
> from the narrow boundaries of our lives,

from the lies that have kept us divided.
Let us re-ignite fires of justice.
Response: **Let us re-ignite fires of justice.**

Let us rise again from ashes . . . How else shall we rise
and re-ignite fires of justice? Tell us.
Let us rise again from ashes . . . *(sharing)*

Diann
L. Neu
Re-igniting fires of justice, let us go forth from this
place to fast from racism, to weep for injustice, to
mourn with ashes, to re-ignite fires of justice. Amen.
Blessed Be. Let It Be So.

76   **Litany**

From peace that is no peace;
from the grip of all that is evil;
from a violent righteousness . . .   **deliver us.**

From paralysis of will;
from lies and misnaming;
from terror of truth . . .   **deliver us.**

From hardness of heart;
from trading in slaughter;
from the worship of death . . .   **deliver us.**

By the folly of your gospel;
by your choosing of our flesh;
by your nakedness and pain . . .   **heal us.**

By your weeping over the city;
by your refusal of the sword;
by your facing of horror . . .   **heal us.**

Janet
Morley
By your bursting from the tomb;
by your coming in judgement;
by your longing for peace . . .   **heal us.**

77   **The way of forgiveness**

Written at the
time of the Gulf
War.

When the story is told
of enemy atrocities
and our own abuses of human rights

how shall we forgive?
how shall we learn to live?

In the aftermath of war
in the exaltation of success
and the bitterness of defeat

how shall we forgive?
how shall we learn to live?

When lives are spent,
cities derelict, the land destroyed
and the cost is reckoned

how shall we forgive?
how shall we learn to live?

When we are confronted with terror
and evil done in the name of justice;
when we are torn by anger and shame

Jan   how shall we forgive?
Berry   how shall we learn to live?

78   **Prayer of intercession**

Holy God, as you have touched us, may we
now touch others with your love

The oppressed and the persecuted,
crying out for the liberating touch of justice

Touch them with your justice in us

The poor and the outcast,
crying out for the life-giving touch of compassion

Touch them with your compassion in us

The battered victims of war and violence,
crying out for the healing touch of peace

Touch them with your peace in us

The lost and the lonely,
crying out for the welcoming touch of friendship

Touch them with your friendship in us

The prisoners of their own fear and cruelty,
crying out for the generous touch of mercy

Touch them with your mercy in us

And those we love,
crying out for the continuing touch of love

Touch them with your love in us

May our lives be the place where you touch us,
and we touch others in your name,
for you are the source of our life and love.

*Kathy
Galloway*   **Amen.**

⁷⁹   **Prayer of confession**

Prepared at the
first Methodist
Consultation for
Women Ministers,
Charney Manor,
Oxford,
September 1984.

God our Creator,
we come to confess that we have failed;
we have not made room for sisters
and brothers to be themselves;
we have rejected the space you have made for us,
and clung to the narrow limits
imposed by false expectations;

we have treated with distaste the delicate,
beautiful workings of our bodies.

For our failure to accept what we are,
our refusal to allow our bodies to speak to our minds
    and our spirits,
our inability to cope with being made in the image of
    God –

Gracious and accepting God, forgive us.

For our failure to accept the pain of others,
our refusal to stand alongside the hurt of other women,
our timidity and cowardice in the face of oppression
    and evil,

Gracious and accepting God, forgive us.

Help us to start again, accepting with joy
our whole humanity, made in your image,
so that we offer our mind, spirit, and body
to be a living sacrifice to your glory.

Rosemary
Wakelin **Amen.**

80 **We lay our broken world**

We lay our broken world
In sorrow at your feet;
Haunted by hunger, war and fear,
Oppressed by power and hate.

Where human life seems less
Than profit, might and pride,
There to unite us all in you,
You lived, and loved, and died.

We bring our broken towns,
Our neighbours hurt and bruised;
You show us how old pain and wounds
For new life can be used.

We bring our broken hopes
For lives of dignity;
Workless and overworked, you love,
And call us to be free.

We bring our broken loves,
Friends parted, families torn;
Then in your life and death we see
That love must be reborn.

We bring our broken selves,
Confused and closed and tired;
Then through your gift of healing grace
New purpose is inspired.

66.86 (Short
metre)
(Many tunes are
suitable, e.g.
Franconia)

Come fill us, fire of God,
Our life and strength renew;

Anna
Briggs

Find in us love, and hope, and trust,
And lift us up to you.

81   **God of justice and peace**

Oxford Women's
Liturgy, March
1986.

God of justice and peace,
You stand with those who are poor,
You ask us women to be the voice of the voiceless.
We call upon you
For those who have suffered the injustice of war and
      greed,
From the depths of our being we cry to you.

(Space for bidding prayers)

. . . Lord, hear us,
Lord, graciously hear us.

Creator God, you know what we need without our
words. Hear our prayers and hear also our silence.
Give us strength. Grant us those things we cannot
or dare not voice. We make all our prayers through
our brother Jesus.

Amen.

82   **The remembrance of them**

O Christ,
in whose body was named
all the violence of the world,
and in whose memory is contained
our profoundest grief,

we lay open to you:
the violence done to us in time before memory;
the unremembered wounds that have misshaped our
        lives;
the injuries we cannot forget and have not forgiven.

The remembrance of them is grievous to us;
the burden of them is intolerable.

We lay open to you:
the violence done in our name in time before memory;
the unremembered wounds we have inflicted;
the injuries we cannot forget and for which we have
        not been forgiven.

The remembrance of them is grievous to us;
the burden of them is intolerable.

We lay open to you:
the victims of violence whose only memorial is our
anger;
those whose suffering was sustained on our behalf;
those whose continued oppression provides the ground
we stand on.

The remembrance of them is grievous to us;
the burden of them is intolerable.

Hear what comfortable words our saviour Christ says
to all who truly turn to God:

Come to me, all you who labour and are heavy-laden,
and I will give you rest.
Take my yoke upon you, and learn of me,
for I am gentle and lowly in heart,
Janet and you will find rest for your souls.
Morley For my yoke is easy, and my burden is light.

83 **A litany of penitence**

Service of
rejoicing for the
fortieth
anniversary of the
ordination of
Florence Li Tim
Oi, Sheffield
Cathedral, January
1984.

O God, whose longing is to reconcile the whole
universe inside your love, pour out your abundant
mercy on your Church, and on your world so
fragmented and torn apart.

For the long history of the pain and travail, of
oppression and prejudice inflicted on women,
within the Church and in the world,

O God, forgive us and pour out your mercy.

For our failure to be open and responsive to the
possibility of new freedoms and new hopes,

O God, forgive us and pour out your mercy.

For our failure to resist the bitterness which poisons
and sours the gospel of love and reconciliation,

O God, forgive us and pour out your mercy.

For our failure to present a wounded world with hope
for reconciliation in a true and loving community of
women and men,

O God, forgive us and pour out your mercy.

O God, whose longing is to reconcile the whole
universe inside your love, pour out your abundant
mercy on your Church and your world so fragmented
and torn apart. This we plead through the love of Jesus
Christ which already surrounds us.

Amen.

84   **Confession**

For a service of
dedication of a
chaplain in the
water industry.

O God, Creator of all that lives,
You have called us to carry the water of life to a
    thirsty world.
We confess with shame
that we have divided and diverted the river of life,
so that the power of your word is wasted and
    weakened;
Lord, we confess
Our life is dry.

We confess that we have forgotten that the water of
    baptism
is the same water that drives the turbine
and irrigates the field;
Lord, we confess
Our life is dry.

We confess that we have dammed up the gospel in
     our churches,
and polluted the oceans of your truth,
so that those who thirst for the water of liberation
have no access to it;
Lord, we confess
Our life is dry.

We confess that we have failed so often
to turn the water of life into the wine of the
     Kingdom;
Lord, we confess
Our life is dry.

Living God, forgive us,
For the sake of your son Jesus Christ our Lord.

God of Love,
we open ourselves and our work
to your rain of love.
We thank you for calling us to share in your work of
     creation.
Come in the power of your Spirit
to make us worthy carriers
Alison   of the water of life,
Norris   to the glory of Christ our Lord.

85 **Strange virtues**

Let our anger be a blessing,
Liberty for minds once numb;
Freedom from the old temptation
To indifference to succumb.
Take the energy it gives us,
Fire to build a world restored;
Overturn the changers' tables,
Cleanse our hearts to hear your word.

Make impatience be our calling,
For a time when all will share
And preserve earth's rich resources,
Freed from powerless despair.
Lift the blinkers that constrain us,
Give us courage to be free;
Warn the hypocrite inside us
To reject complacency.

Let the soul that feels forsaken,
Wronged, deserted, scorned, and lost,
Feel the keenness of oppression
Wrought by some at others' cost;
Use each hurt to teach compassion,
Draw us where the weakest cry;
With your nail-marked hands enfold us,
Show us love will never die.

Angry, hurt, impatient Jesus,
By your life and lonely death,
Take our deepest feelings, fill them,
Through your Spirit's healing breath.
Thus inspired by anger, sorrow,
And impatient for your reign,

Anna To your resurrection call us,
Briggs Heal our world with love again.

86 **Hymn for Transition House Sunday**

Written for use in
the United
Churches in
Canada when
their Sunday
worship took
domestic violence
and abuse as a
theme.

You gave us to each other, Lord,
In love to live and grow,
One flesh created, giving life,
Delight and trust to know.

With grace for joy and constancy
You bless each human soul,
To mirror your self-giving love,
Make mind and body whole.

But anguished cries now rise to you
From hearts betrayed and shamed,
By lashing tongue and thrusting fist,
And touch unasked, un-named.

The hands you made for tender care,
Love's openness to tell,
Strip self-esteem, wreak fear and death,
Make home a hidden hell.

Stretch out your nail-marked hands in love,
Make violence to cease;
Heal those whose cruel acts and words
Destroy their loved ones' peace.

C.M.
recommended
tune: St Flavian

Restore the homes deprived of joy,
Deliver those in pain,

Anna
Briggs

Bring justice, liberty from fear,
And hope to live again.

⁸⁷ **In a circle**

Written for Brian
MacLeod, who
died of AIDS,
2.3.88.

You called us all to you
And like moths round a flame,
How we timidly flew
While we first learned your name;
We hung back and trembled,
At the pain we might share;
But found, once assembled,
We were safe in your care.

The gifts that you gave us,
Unexpected and free,
Were the gifts that would save us
From the worst we could be;
Your suffering face
Brought our striving release;
Your patience and grace
Gave our busy lives peace.

In a thousand new ways
The world nails you again,
Deserts and betrays,
Yet you love through your pain.
Each nail mark inflicted
By our failure to see
Restores us, convicted,
Forgiven and free.

And the circle drawn round you
Wakes the barriers to move,
As we see each one's face
In the light of your love;
Through your suffering you healed
Our division and pain,
Through your dying you sealed
A community's name.

Now the wounded one makes
A community live,
And indifference shakes
As we learn how to give.
The one at the centre
Bids us turn from our strife,
And calls us to enter
And rejoice in new life.

Tune: Scottish
traditional: 'When
look to the high
ills'.

Anna
Briggs

⁸⁸ **We love you, Lord**

We love you, Lord, but doubt the truth
That love lives on, though crucified,
Unless we see your broken hands
And touch your scarred and wounded side.

We hear the stories others tell,
The words you spoke, the bread you brake;

Unless we see you rise ourselves
We find commitment hard to make.

Now put our fingers in the wounds:
The world, your body, nailed again;
Your lonely, suffering, outcast ones
Who dare to live in hope through pain;

Where justice beckons in the hearts
Of those denied the right to be;
Where faith endures the trial and sword,
And calls a people to be free;

Where those despised, oppressed, ignored
For colour, gender, mind and age,
Find their self-confidence restored,
And freedom from destructive rage;

Tune: Angelus

Where dying people find your peace
And laughter lights the ones who grieve,

Anna

Where healing bonds of care increase,

Briggs

We see your marks, and we believe.

⁸⁹ **Prayer for wholeness**

O God,
Giver of Life
Bearer of Pain
Maker of Love,
you are able to accept in us what we
cannot even acknowledge;
you are able to name in us what we
cannot bear to speak of;
you are able to hold in your memory
what we have tried to forget;
you are able to hold out to us
the glory that we cannot conceive of.
Reconcile us through your cross

to all that we have rejected in our selves,
that we may find no part of your creation
to be alien or strange to us,
and that we ourselves may be made whole.

Through Jesus Christ, our lover and our friend.

Janet
Morley   **Amen.**

90   **Christmas crib**

Before the crib I kneel to pray:
Still centre of a rocking, reeling world.
This child, this mother and man
Here strip me, show me as I am.

Before the child I kneel to pray:
Still centre of my rocking, aching heart.
Child in me, alone, bereft of mother,
Here grieve and gain the family I can't recover.

Before the mother I kneel to pray:
Still centre of my rocking, yearning heart.
Mother in me unmade, bereft of child,
Here grieve and gain the babe I'll never have.

Beside the man I kneel to pray:
Still centre of my rocking, wounded heart.
Lover in me undone, bereft of lover,
Here grieve and gain the passion that is over.

Before the three I kneel to pray:
Still centre of a rocking, reeling world.
Nicola   Child, mother, man in me I offer
Slee   The gift of costly love which first I see here proffered.

⁹¹ **From women in ministry to priests of the Church
of England**

Brothers, we love you.
We have shared in your glowing times of joy
and given thanks with you;
we have prayed the Spirit down on you
and knelt for your blessing;
we have watched you bowing awestruck at the altar
and adored with you;
we have stood with you by a child's grave
and wept with you.

Brothers, we love you.
We have felt how tenderly you care
and we trust you;
we have listened to you
and learned from you;
we have heard you wrestling with questions
and we respect you;
we have seen you stand for truth and justice
and we honour you.

Brothers, we love you.
We have opened our griefs to you
and been healed by your comfort;
you have wounded us, and we have sensed the pain
behind the blow
and suffered with you.
We have hurt you, slighted you, burdened you, blamed
you, taken you for granted
and you have forgiven us –
and so you have done to us
and we have forgiven you.

Brothers, we love you.
We have teased you, laughed with you, played with
you, punctured your self-importance
and nurtured your self-worth.

We have found you doubting, bruised, exhausted,
        afraid, despairing,
                        and held you in our hearts.
We have fought you, argued with you, passionately
        opposed you,
                        and begged to be your sisters.

Rosemary   Brothers, we love you.
CHN   Will you welcome us?

92   **Prayer**

Go-between God:
inweave the fabric of our common life,
Jennifer that the many-coloured beauty of your love
Wild   may find expression in all our exchanges.

⁹³ **Blessing the bread**

<table>
<tr><td>A litany for four</td><td>1</td><td>In the beginning was God</td></tr>
<tr><td>voices, written for</td><td>2</td><td>In the beginning, the source of all that is</td></tr>
<tr><td>International</td><td>3</td><td>In the beginning, God, yearning</td></tr>
<tr><td>Women's Year,</td><td>4</td><td>God, moaning</td></tr>
<tr><td>Washington DC,</td><td>1</td><td>God, labouring</td></tr>
<tr><td>USA, Spring</td><td>2</td><td>God, giving birth</td></tr>
<tr><td>1978.</td><td>3</td><td>God, rejoicing</td></tr>
</table>

4   And God loved what she had made
1   And God said, 'It is good.'

2   Then God, knowing that all that is good is shared
3   Held the earth tenderly in her arms
4   God yearned for relationship
1   God longed to share the good earth
2   And humanity was born in the yearning of God
3   We were born to share the earth

4   In the earth was the seed
1   In the seed was the grain
2   In the grain was the harvest
3   In the harvest was the bread
4   In the bread was the power

1   And God said, All shall eat of the earth
2   All shall eat of the seed
3   All shall eat of the grain
4   All shall eat of the harvest
1   All shall eat of the bread
2   All shall eat of the power

3   God said, You are my people
4   My friends
1   My lovers
2   My sisters
3   And brothers
4   All of you shall eat
1   Of the bread

2   And the power
3   All shall eat

4   Then God, gathering up her courage in love,
         said,
1   Let there be bread!
2   And God's sisters, her friends and lovers, knelt
         on the earth
3   planted the seeds
4   prayed for the rain
1   sang for the grain
2   made the harvest
3   cracked the wheat
4   pounded the corn
1   kneaded the dough
2   kindled the fire
3   filled the air with the smell of fresh bread
4   And there was bread!
1   And it was good!

2   We, the sisters of God, say today
3   All shall eat of the bread,
4   And the power,
1   We say today,
2   All shall have power
3   And bread.
4   Today we say
1   Let there be bread.
2   And let there be power!
3   Let us eat of the bread and the power!
4   And all will be filled
1   For the bread is rising!

2   By the power of God
3   Women are blessed
4   By the women of God
1   The bread is blessed
2   By the bread of God
3   The power is blessed
4   By the power of bread

1   The power of women
2   The power of God
3   The people are blessed

1, 2, 3, 4

Carter   The earth is blessed
Heyward   **And the bread is rising.**

94   Coming down to earth

In the breadshop,
among homely smells
and human conversations,
I started to weep with joy:
for the dailiness of bread
and shared meals,

Jan   people meeting and needs met,
Sutch   the sacraments
Pickard   of love and laughter.

95   Prayer of thanksgiving

Prepared at the   By your creative word, O Eternal Wisdom,
first Methodist   you established us
Consultation for   and all things living in your saving Presence;
Women
Ministers,   You sent Moses to free your people
Charney Manor,   from slavery in Egypt,
Oxford,   and he drew courage from your promise:
September 1984.   'I will be with you.'

To Mary your promise was:
'Hail, favoured one, the Lord is with you.'
And by the overshadowing of the Holy Spirit
the Word became flesh and dwelt among us.

Therefore with the whole creation,
existing for your glory,
with the minds you have filled with your purpose;
with the bodies you have given us as women and men
and the hearts you have inflamed with love;
with Eve, the mother of us all,
with Sarah, Deborah, and Miriam, and
all who lived by faith in the promise of freedom;
with Mary who bore your son and Anna who
        recognized him,
with Mary Magdalen who found his grave empty,
with prophets, apostles and saints of every generation,
we proclaim your great and glorious name,
forever praising you and saying:

Holy, holy, holy, God of power and might;
heaven and earth are full of your glory;
Hosanna in the highest.

96   **Fruit of the earth and work of human hands**

Heads bowed,
Stalks cut,
Ears threshed,
Grain crushed,
White flour.

Head bowed,
Fingers working,
Yeast – flour
Dough rising,
Bread cooked.

We offer you, Father,
        this bread,
Fruit of the earth
And work of human hands.
Blessed be God forever.

Heads bowed,
Bread no more.
Christ's Body
Given for all.

Heads bowed,
Daily bread
Held in hand,
Life's strand,
God enfleshed.

Anne
Hine   **Amen.**

97   **The feast of Life**

Come on,
let us celebrate the supper of the Lord.
Let us make a huge loaf of bread
and let us bring abundant wine
like at the wedding at Cana.

Let the women not forget the salt.
Let the men bring along the yeast.
Let many guests come,
the lame, the blind, the crippled, the poor.

Come quickly.
Let us follow the recipe of the Lord.
All of us, let us knead the dough together
with our hands.
Let us see with joy
how the bread grows.

Because today
we celebrate
the meeting with the Lord.
Today we renew our commitment
Elsa   **to the Kingdom.**
Tamez   **Nobody will stay hungry.**

⁹⁸   Blessing over a meal prepared together

In the beginning, God created the heavens and the earth.
The earth was without form, and void, and darkness was
upon the face of the deep, and the Spirit of God was
brooding upon the face of the waters. (Genesis 1.1–2)

O dearest Spirit of God,
you brood over our deep places,
our darkness, and our chaos;
you embrace us with your power to create;
you stir in us a desire to grow.
Stay with us
in our darkness and in our insight,
in our formless thoughts, and in
those we can express,
in our chaotic emotions,
and in our new becoming.

We give you thanks
for this food which is our life,
for the fruits of the earth,
conceived in darkness,
rooted in the secret soil.
We offer you our part in the mess of creativity.
We wash, prepare, cook, present;
we eat, and taste, and enjoy with our bodies;
we clear away the mess.

Janet   We embrace with you the chaos that fulfils,
Morley   the secret labour that maintains life.

⁹⁹   Did the woman say?

Did the woman say,
When she held him for the first time in the
      dark dank of a stable,
After the pain and the bleeding and the crying,
        'This is my body; this is my blood'?

Did the woman say,
When she held him for the last time in the
    dark rain on a hilltop,
After the pain and the bleeding and the dying,
       'This is my body; this is my blood'?

Well that she said it to him then,
For dry old men,

Frances   Brocaded robes belying barrenness,
Croake Frank   Ordain that she not say it for him now.

100   **Eucharist**

Lord Jesus,

thank you for inviting us to your table,
for here, you show us our lives

       the daily bread of our work and care
       the wine of delight, pressed from the fruits
       of our creativity
       and our brokenness, with all its pain
       and appalled self-knowledge.

We celebrate the life that is ours,
for your eternal word is
that it is precious in your sight.

And here you offer us your life,

       broken to share life
       poured out to renew life
       promised to transform life.

We celebrate the life that is yours
pattern of reality for us.

And here, your life and our lives

become one in spirit and in flesh
moving out into the life of the world.

We celebrate the life that is
          love revealed
          love given and received
          love in action.

Kathy
Galloway

101   **Fraction prayers for Christmas 1992**

'East' and 'South'
passages are
spoken by the
celebrant; 'West'
and 'North' by
the deacon. A
fraction takes
place after each
section, the
speaker(s) moving
round the altar,
stopping at each
direction. The
congregation is
(usually) in a circle
round the altar.
These prayers
were originally
written for St
James' Church,
Piccadilly,
London.

We break this bread to the East
for all who on this holy night
and at all other times

worship you, O God of many names,
amongst us in all faiths.

Who once upon a most ancient time
broke all loveless laws,
all bloody histories, all barren cultures,

that in the birth of the child Jesus

we who are many and benighted
may see again clearly your great glory
and sing with one voice your praise, O God,
most holy Maker of all.

We break this bread to the South
for the earth
which on this holy night
despite the pollution of plenty
and the plunder of poverty

sings of your mercy and compassion
in giving us the good grace
of Jesus your child

that we may confess and repent,
repair and return

to the stable home
of your most holy wholeness,
made flesh and among us
in a baby amidst beasts of burden.

We break this bread to the West
in joyous thanksgiving

that on this, Christ's holy birth night,
in blood and pain
you shared yourself
with all your world

that we may do likewise.

We break this bread to the North
in awe and praise upon this holy night
at the great light of your salvation
which shone forth at Bethlehem

that we, in whom hope grows dim,
dreams fade,
through sins
of greed or sloth or hate

Puck   may again receive
de Raadt   Your coming in Christ's gentle glory.

102   **The Word is made flesh**

Leader: The Word was made flesh and lived among
          us
ALL: **FULL OF GRACE AND TRUTH, HE
          LIVED AMONG US**

Leader: When the glory of a sunset makes
              worshippers of people
          When the High Street becomes holy ground
          When there is room for things to grow
ALL: **THE WORD IS MADE FLESH AND
          LIVES AMONG US**

Leader: In attentive silence to another's story
          In the first steps taken in forgiveness
          In a disguise able to be left aside
ALL: **THE WORD IS MADE FLESH AND
          LIVES AMONG US**

Leader: In good bread on the table
          In the loving embrace of a friend
          In tears of anger for a homeless child
ALL: **THE WORD IS MADE FLESH AND
          LIVES AMONG US**

Leader: In a secret shared with confidence
          In a child listened to with respect
          In care that does not draw back from shame
ALL: **THE WORD IS MADE FLESH AND
          LIVES AMONG US**

Leader: When we put our money where our mouths
              are
          When theory becomes practice
          When intentions become actions
ALL: **THE WORD IS MADE FLESH AND
          LIVES AMONG US**

Leader: When the Word is made flesh and lives
among us

Kathy
Galloway *ALL:* **SATAN HAS NO POWER**

103 Blessing of bread

This and the
following piece
are taken from a
liturgy originally
celebrated during
the harvest
season, but
adaptable 'to any
season until war
ceases'.

Blessed are you, Holy One of Peace, for you promise
your people food for the journey, nourishment for
the struggle.

Blessed are you, Holy One of Peace, for you sent your
people manna as they wandered in the desert.

Blessed are you, Holy One of Peace, for you are the
bread of life.

Blessed are you, Holy One of Peace, give us this day
our daily bread, the bread of freedom from war,
the bread of peace for all peoples.

Blessed are you, Holy One of Peace, for you taught
our mothers to bake this bread. Fill us with the
rising power of this bread.

Blessed are you, Holy One of Peace, for you keep us
hungry for a world without war.

Let us extend our hands, palms up, and bless this bread.

Diann
L. Neu Blessed are you, Holy One of Peace, bless this bread
with your gifts of peace.

104 Blessing of fruit of the vine

Blessed are you, Holy One of the Harvest, for you
invite us to come and drink deeply.

Blessed are you, Holy One of the Harvest, for you beg
us to drink this fruit of the vine in memory of all
who have died for peace.

Blessed are you, Holy One of the Harvest, for you help
us to remember women's lives, women's blood,

women who have been killed, martyred, raped and
wounded at the time of war.
Blessed are you, Holy One of the Harvest, for even
though we drink, you keep us thirsty for peace.
Blessed are you, Holy One of the Harvest, refresh us
with a firm and daring spirit.
Blessed are you, Holy One of the Harvest, for you
create the fruit of the vine and show us the way
to liberation.
Let us extend our hands, palms up, and bless this fruit
of the vine.

Diann   Blessed are you, Holy One of the Harvest, bless this
L. Neu   wine and juice with your gifts of peace.

¹⁰⁵   **Rest at the reflecting pool**

ent to WATER
Women's
lliance for
heology, Ethics
d Ritual) donors
a 1993 year
d/1994 year
ginning
essing.

Preparation

*Pick your favorite bowl, put it in a special place and fill it
with water. Use rose water, ocean water, spring water, or
tap water with desired additives: salt, herbs, a few drops of
oil, a flower, or vegetable coloring for a seasonal theme.
Choose a quiet time of day, or perhaps once a month when
the moon is full, to rest.*
   *Invite a friend or several to join you if you like. Put on
music if you wish. Rest your body in a comfortable place
and relax.*

Centering

*Look into the water and calm yourself.
Come, rest at the reflecting pool.*
         Blessed are you, Holy Wisdom,
               for bringing rest to my body.
         Blessed are you, Well of Stillness,
               for surrounding me with calm.

Blessing

Dip your hands into the water.
Touch your forehead saying,
      Bless me, Holy Wisdom,
          and bring rest to my body.
Touch your heart saying,
      Bless my heart and rest my loving.
Touch your eyes saying,
      Bless my eyes and rest my seeing.
Touch your ears saying,
      Bless my ears and rest my hearing.
Touch your mouth saying,
      Bless my mouth and rest my speaking.
Touch your breasts (or where your breasts used to be) saying,
      Bless my breasts and rest my nurturing.
Touch your womb (or where your womb used to be) saying,
      Bless my womb and rest my creating.
Touch your hands saying,
      Bless my hands and rest my touching.
Touch your feet saying,
      Bless my feet and rest my walking.
Take a deep breath and exhale saying,
      Bless me, Holy Wisdom, and bring me rest.

Reflection

Pause and enjoy your restful state for as long as you desire.
Think about how you incorporate times of pause into your
daily/monthly schedule. Imagine how you will take time to
rest tomorrow/this month.
    Take time now to meditate, write in a journal, converse,
draw, dance or do something else that gives you pleasure.

Closing

Look into the water and calm yourself.
Go forth, refreshed from the reflecting pool.

Blessed are you, Holy Wisdom,
    for bringing rest to my body.
Blessed are you, Well of Stillness,
    for surrounding me with calm.

Diann
L. Neu
and
Mary E.
Hunt

Drink from the water of your reflecting pool and/or pour it
    around your plants.

106   **Eucharistic prayer for Christmas Eve**

This was
originally written
for a women's
Eucharist at Holy
Trinity House,
Paddington.

O Eternal Wisdom,
we praise you and give you thanks,
because you emptied yourself of power
and became foolishness for our sake:
for on this night you were delivered as one of us,
a baby needy and naked,
wrapped in a woman's blood;
born into poverty and exile,
to proclaim the good news to the poor,
and to let the broken victims go free.

Therefore, with the woman who gave you birth,
the women who befriended you and fed you,
who argued with you and touched you,
the woman who anointed you for death,
the women who met you, risen from the dead,
and with all your lovers throughout the ages,
we praise you, saying:

Holy, holy, holy,
vulnerable God,
heaven and earth are full of your glory;
hosanna in the highest.
Blessed is the one
who comes in the name of God;
hosanna in the highest.

Blessed is our brother Jesus,

bone of our bone and flesh of our flesh;
who, on the night when he was delivered over to
      death,
took bread, gave thanks, broke it, and said:
'This is my body, which is for you.
Do this to remember me.'
In the same way also the cup, after supper, saying:
'This cup is the new covenant in my blood.
Do this, whenever you drink it,
to remember me.'
For, as we eat this bread and drink this cup,
we are proclaiming the Lord's death until he comes.

Christ has died.
Christ is risen.
Christ will come again.

Come now, dearest Spirit of God,
embrace us with your comfortable power.
Brood over these bodily things,
and make us one body in Christ.
As Mary's body was broken for him,
and her blood shed,
so may we show forth his brokenness,
for the life of the world,
Janet   and may creation be made whole
Morley   through the new birth in his blood.

107   **That night we gathered**

This poem was
written after, and
celebrates, the
service for which
the previous
eucharistic prayer
was written.

That night we gathered for the birth, as women
have always done – as women
have never done till now;
and in an ordinary room,
warm, exposed, and intimate as childbed,
we spoke about our bodies and our blood,
waiting for God's delivery:
silence, gesture, and speech

announcing, with a strange appropriate blend
of mystery and bluntness,

Janet
Morley

the celebration of the word made flesh
midwived wholly by women.

¹⁰⁸ **A wilderness liturgy**

outhwark
Vomen Seeking
Ordination
roup, Petertide,
utside
outhwark
athedral during
e ordination
rvice, 3 July
83.

She who would valiant be
'Gainst all disaster
Let her in constancy
    Follow the Master.
There's no discouragement
Shall make her once relent
Her first avowed intent
To be a pilgrim.

Who so beset her round
With dismal stories,
Do but themselves confound –
    Her strength the more is.
No foes shall stay her might
Though she with giants fight!
She will make good her right
To be a pilgrim.

ohn Bunyan,
tered)

Since, Lord, thou dost defend
Us with thy Spirit,
We know we at the end
    Shall life inherit.
Then fancies flee away!
I'll fear not what men say,
I'll labour night and day
To be a pilgrim.

Old Testament Reading: Exodus 19.2–6

Hymn: Tell out my soul, the greatness of the Lord

New Testament Reading: 1 Peter 2.4–10

Sermon

Intercessions

O Living God, we pray for your holy people, the
      Church. We ask that every member may be freed
      to serve you in truth and grace.
We remember our foremothers. We remember all
      women who have recognized that to be a person
      of faith is to respond in action. We give thanks:
For Miriam, poetess of the Exodus, leader through the
      wilderness;
For Deborah, a mother and a judge in Israel;
For Rachel, traveller with Jacob;
For the woman who bathed Jesus' feet with her tears;
For Mary Magdalene, first apostle of the resurrection.

We give you thanks, O God.

Let us remember all those women who have faced the
      unknown in faith and met fear with courage. We
      give thanks:
For all those women who have dared to step forward
      and lead;
For all those women who have challenged the
      stereotypes of society and risked standing alone.

We give you thanks, O God.

Let us remember women who have struggled to reform
      our history, who have sought in their time to
      minister to the needs of the hurt, the disadvantaged
      and the alienated in our land. We give thanks:
For Florence Nightingale, Elizabeth Fry, the Pankhursts,
      Josephine Butler and, above all, for all those
      without a name.

We give you thanks, O God.

We pray for those, known and unknown, who have
　　laboured in the struggle before us. We give
　　thanks:
For Maude Royden, Phoebe Willetts, Mollie Batten,
　　Elsie Chamberlain, Una Kroll, Revd Florence Li
　　Tim Oi.

We give you thanks, O God.

**O holy and sustaining God, make us worthy to
inherit their valour and vision. Challenge us again
lest we wither and perish by holding to the
familiar when it has lost its savour. As your
daughters and sons, may we be brought nearer
to a new vision of your love, through the grace of
the Holy Spirit. Amen.**

The wilderness meal

The Israelites complained to Moses and Aaron in the
wilderness and said, 'If only we had died at Yahweh's
hand in Egypt, where we sat round the fleshpots and
had plenty of bread to eat! But you have brought us
out into this wilderness to let this whole assembly
starve to death!'

　　Moses and Aaron then said to all the Israelites, 'In
the evening you will know that it was Yahweh who
brought you out of Egypt, and in the morning you will
see the glory of Yahweh, because he has heeded your
complaints against him; it is not against us that you
bring your complaints; we are nothing.'

　　That evening a flock of quails flew in and settled
all over the camp, and in the morning a fall of dew lay
all around it. When the dew was gone, there in the
wilderness, fine flakes appeared as hoar frost on the
ground. Moses said to them, 'That is the bread which
Yahweh has given you to eat.'

The honey cake is handed round.

Israel called the food manna; it was white, like coriander seed, and it tasted like a wafer made with honey.

'This', said Moses, 'is the command which Yahweh has given: Take a full omer of it to be kept for future generations, so that they may see the bread with which I fed you in the wilderness when I brought you out of Egypt.'

The Israelites ate the manna for forty years until they came to a land where they could settle; they ate it until they came to the frontier of the land of Canaan.

Reading from Isaiah 66.5–13

Hear the word of Yahweh, you who revere his word: Your fellow countrymen who hate you, who spurn you because you bear my name, have said, 'Let Yahweh show his glory, then we shall see you rejoice'; but they shall be put to shame. That roar from the city, that uproar in the temple, is the sound of Yahweh's dealing retribution to his foes.

Shall a woman bear a child without pains? Give birth to a son before the onset of labour? Who has heard of anything like this? Who has seen any such thing? Shall a country be born after one day's labour, shall a nation be brought to birth all in a moment? But Zion, at the onset of her pangs, bore her children. Shall I bring to the point of birth and not deliver? Yahweh says: Shall I who deliver close the womb? Your God has spoken.

The milk is passed round.

Rejoice with Jerusalem and exult in her, all you who love her; share her joy with all your heart, all you who mourn over her. Then you may suck and be fed from her breasts that give comfort, delighting in her plentiful milk. For thus says Yahweh: 'I will send peace flowing over her like a river, and the wealth of nations like a stream in flood; she shall suckle you and you shall be carried in her arms and dandled on her knees. As a

mother comforts her child, so will I myself comfort
you, and you shall find comfort in Jerusalem.'

Hymn: Come, thou holy Paraclete

The covenant between us — from Ruth 1.16–18

'Where you go, I will go, and where you stay, I will
    stay.
Your people shall be my people, and your God my
    God.
Where you die, I will die, and there I will be buried.
I swear a solemn oath before Yahweh your God:
    nothing but death shall divide us.'

We offer the sign of peace.

109 **Christmas**

God our midwife . . .
Contain in your hands
the breaking of waters,
the blood and the din of your birth:
then, through our tears and joy, deliverer,
Gill your wrinkled, infant kingdom may be born.
Paterson **Amen.**

110 **A design of Beauty**

Though winter covers
    our Earth
and cold frost stunts
    much growth,
Yet the Hope of Spring
is awakening us.

For we all are the saplings
Marianne God has planted, watered
Adjei   and nurtured.
and
Lala We are God's handiwork
Winkley   a design of Beauty.

111 **Nativity**

Something starts to shift,
to move; to prove
I am not dead. Something
stirs inside my head.
The blood runs deep and red.
The pulse is firm and strong.
It will not be long
till she is born, till she is

bled, the life kicked
sheer out of me in one great
tear, the flesh giving way in its
war against her own
unstoppable, unbiddable
    child.
       Child of my body,
she will emerge, bloodied but whole,
naked and tender as any
newborn, but fearless, resilient,
perfectly formed. Child of my flesh,
she will thrash her vigorous
limbs, she will fill her
young, never-tried lungs
thick with the fast approaching
air. And with one primeval
scream, she'll rend the void and

Nicola utter her first wordless, miraculous
Slee
                  Word.

112 **Epiphany**
     Upon the ending of a long marriage

'Today is my epiphany'

This is the turning point.
Change is coming
the door stands wide
and there is no just cause
or impediment
why I should not walk through
into the liberation
of the place beyond

I choose
freedom
now
I follow

my star
wherever
it may   I choose
lead   dissolution
                   of false hope
                        dependency
                        security

I,   , take thee, spirit of truth
to be my lodestar,
in sickness and in health
for richer and for poorer
forsaking all other
I pledge my journey
Jean   to follow you
Clark   all the days of my life.

¹¹³ **Conversations with Muse (3)**

Dare to
declare
who you
are. It
isn't
far from
the shores
of silence
to the
boundaries
of speech.
The road
is not
long but
the way
is deep.
And you
must not

only
walk there,
you must
Nicola be prepared
Slee to leap.

114 **Transition (Mode Transformative)**
Human

his is the fourth
f a sequence of
ve poems
ntitled
ollectively
Virgin Birth'.

Can't go forward
Can't go back
Can't go home
Can't go out
Can't cross over
Can't stay here
This is time
This is no time
This is place
This is no place.
This is choice
This is no choice
Help me
Don't help me
Hold me
Don't hold me
Tell me
Don't tell me
Intersection
Interface
Inter-ruption
It's no good.
Stuck.
Have to
transpose
into a
different key
explode

on to a
different plane
expand
on to a
different dimension.

Kathy   Yes.
Galloway   Now we're in business.

¹¹⁵   **Wrestler**

This, this is the place.
Seek love here, where
love is displaced,
overcome by fear. Dare

to look again. Face
again the stark wall
that blocks out all space.
Welcome dark. Fall

to fear that gives you chase.
Clasp your foe, hold
him in fierce embrace,
nor let him go. Fold

him to your chaste-
ned, beaten heart. Wrest
the blessing from his grace-
less lips. At once depart, lest

he should mark the face
turned to receive his gaze. Go,
Nicola   hasten from this place.
Slee   The wound will always show.

On leaving the church, 4 December 1989

An extract from a
statement made by
the author to
fellow members of
her church
congregation on
the occasion of her
leaving the church.

This is not easy for me. But I did not want to leave without saying goodbye face to face. I did not want you to wonder where I had gone and then find that I had just gone and left a note on the kitchen table. I have not been one to hold my tongue in all the time I have been here.

The reasons for my leaving I have written as clearly as I could in the parish paper. However, I want to make it quite clear that I am leaving the church not because I am no longer passionate about the gospel, but because I am; that I am leaving not because I do not love you, but because I do. I am choosing to live my faith outside the church. And in living as an outsider I remain in solidarity with those of you who are brave enough to live your faith inside the church which persists by its words and actions (and inaction) to call you outsiders.

I am going in peace to love and serve my God.

*Linda
Walter*

I will pray for you as I hope you will pray for me.

Epiphany

O God,
who am I now?
Once, I was secure
 in familiar territory
 in my sense of belonging
unquestioning of
 the norms of my culture
 the assumptions built into my language
 the values shared by my society.

But now you have called me out and away from home

and I do not know where you are leading.
I am empty, unsure, uncomfortable.
I have only a beckoning star to follow.

Journeying God,
pitch your tent with mine
so that I may not become deterred
by hardship, strangeness, doubt.
Show me the movement I must make
    toward a wealth not dependent on possessions
    toward a wisdom not based on books
    toward a strength not bolstered by might
    toward a God not confined to heaven
but scandalously earthed, poor, unrecognized . . .

Kate   help me to find myself
Compston   as I walk in others' shoes.

118   **Naming and presentation**
       A dedication

From a sequence,   God of many names,
Prayers for   my name is known to you.
Christmastide.   I am held in the hand of your life,
and I do not know what you will make of me.
All I know is that I cannot make myself
any more than I could in my mother's womb.
But this I can do,
this I choose,
to give myself into the hand of your continuing
    creativity.
My past, with its joys and triumphs, its failures and
    regrets.
My present, with its struggles and accomplishments, its
    failures and regrets.
My future, with its fears and freedom, its pain and
    promise.
To loose and to bind, to stretch and to shape,
to become what I will,

trusting the hand that made the world
trusting the spirit that breathes life

Kathy
Galloway

trusting the love that will not let me go
trusting the promise of the Word made flesh.

¹¹⁹ **Clear the way**

Prayer of the
Ecumenical
Spirituality
Project.

God of surprises
    you call us

        from the narrowness of our traditions to new
            ways of being church
        from the captivities of our culture to creative
            witness for justice
        from the smallness of our horizons to the
            bigness of your vision

ALL: **Clear the way in us, your people,**
        that we might call others to freedom and
            renewed faith.

Jesus, wounded healer,
    you call us

        from preoccupation with our own histories
            and hurts to daily tasks of peacemaking
        from privilege to pilgrimage
        from insularity to inclusive community

ALL: **Clear the way in us, your people,**
        that we might call others to wholeness
            and integrity.

Holy, transforming, Spirit,
    you call us

        from fear to faithfulness
        from clutter to clarity

*Joan
Puls
and
Gwen
Cashmore*

from a desire to control to deeper trust
from the refusal to love to a readiness to risk

ALL: **Clear the way in us, your people,
that we might all know the beauty and power
and danger of the gospel.**

120   **A revelation**

I had never thought language mattered.
After all, my god is beyond gender,
I didn't need all that.

I went to a circle dance group one day:
I centred into the music, into the movement,
Away from the busyness,
Right down into somewhere
Inside myself.

A pause in the music.
The group entered into silence.
The silence was sustained.

Into stillness
A male voice, yet still in the silence.
Words about that which no one can
Fully describe.
The near, yet far —
Spirit, Ground, Force, Love, . . . God . . .
He had said   She

A light feeling came over me
Weight lifted and floated away
Warmth swelled around and filled me.

He had said
She.

June   Only then did I know
Pettitt   it had mattered.

121   **I am a woman**

Just because you are a woman,
They consider you a sinner,
Call you 'weak' by name,
Demand that you be man's loyal follower,
Lock you in the 'prison' of family.
'Femininity' becomes your ornament throughout your
    whole life.

Just because you are a woman,
They have authority to dominate your fate,
Possess your inheritance,
Deprive you of your rights,
Limit your development,
Insult your body,
Damage your esteem.

Yet Jesus Christ listened to women's appeals,
Affirmed a woman's value,
Reproached the tradition that oppresses women.
He made friends with prostitutes,
Talked with heathen women,
Affirmed Mary's choice as good,
Praised the widow's offering.
He affirmed that woman is also created and cared for
    by God.

Therefore, I have decided to accept Jesus Christ as my
    Lord.
I am a woman,
A life that God created and cares about.
I have an independent personality
And the right to choose my way of living.
I have to live out God's image,

Break society's traditional discrimination against
    women,
Rose Share with men God's gospel of liberation,
Wu Manage this world and this land with them.

122 **Not circle dancing**

When I am angry,
I do not want to pour oil on troubled waters,
apologize,
or listen to someone giving me a lecture about how
women are naturally pacifying, reconciling.
I want to get in the ring and go
fifteen rounds with someone who is up to my weight,
then (not minding if I lose) shake hands
and go to the pub.
Failing a worthy opponent,
I want to sweep a large floor,
play a fast game of table tennis,
or swear loudly at the government.
Above all, I do not want to circle dance.
I am a different kind of woman.

When I am hurt,
I do not want to crawl away and lick my wounds;
take myself discreetly out of sight,
hide my pain where it will discomfort no one.
But neither (mostly) do I want somebody else to suffer
'make the bastard pay'.
I want respect.
My own fault it may be
or, life being as it is, maybe not,
nevertheless I want to face it out.

Have people look me in the eye
and know there is no shame in being hurt.
Not disappear, be there.
Have someone hold my hand from time to time;
because they love me, not because I'm hurt.
But I do not want to circle dance.
I am a different kind of woman.

When I am sad,
I do not want to cry or make a noise,
or meditate upon the tragedy of life.
I want to be quite still, and hold my sorrow
carefully within the carved-out hollow in my heart
I keep for it.
And then I want to sing a very powerful song,
catch its heartbeat,
ride with it.
I want to face a complex challenge,
wrestle to give form to words upon an empty sheet of
     paper,
make a plan,
do some work with women.
I do not want to circle dance.
I am a different kind of woman.

When I am happy,
I do not want to buy a dress
or say a prayer,
tell my mother or have a night out with the girls.
I want to have some friends round, make good food,
sit at the table drinking wine by candlelight,
not talk a lot, but listen to the flow
and dance of conversation and exchange.
Or take a journey somewhere with my kids.
Or listen to a street musician playing saxophone among
     the crowds.
Or even dance an eightsome reel.
But not a circle dance (well, perhaps, but I can
take or leave it).
I am a different kind of woman.

Kathy
Galloway

123 **Revelation**

God's work of art.
That's me?
Then beauty must lie
In the eye of the
Beholder.

I feel more like
One of those statues
Michelangelo left
Half emerging
From the marble block;
Full of potential,
On the verge of life,
But prisoned still
By circumstance and
Fear.

Yet part of me is free —
And you are still creating,
Bringing to life
The promise that is there.

Sometimes by
Hammer blows
Which jar my being,
Sometimes by
Tender strokes half felt
Which waken me to
Life.

Go on, Lord.
Love me into wholeness.
Set me free
To share with you
In your creative joy;
To laugh with you
At your delight
Ann   In me,
Lewin Your work of art.

124   Blessed be the New Year

This was sent to
WATER donors
as a 1992/1993
blessing.

Preparation

*Pick your favorite candle and put it in a special place. Or
gather many significant candles and arrange them to please
yourself. Choose a quiet time of the day for your lighting.
Your candle(s) joined with those of others around the world
illuminate new hopes, dispel old fears.*

*Invite a friend or several to join you if you like. Put on
music if you wish. Rest your body in a comfortable place
and relax.*

Centering
[*Light your candle(s)*]
This is the season of hope!
Let the Spirit of Hope surround you.
Let your spirit rise to bless this new year.

Blessing

O Great Spirit of Hope, blessed be your holy seasons.
Blessed be this season when we move to a new year.
Blessed be this magical time for new beginnings and
fond farewells.
Blessed be this 'crack between the worlds' that we
encounter at the New Year.
Blessed be this threshold place of transition between
inside and outside.
Blessed be this transformation when spirits of hope and
change gather.
Blessed be this passage from past securities to uncharted
uncertainties.
Blessed be this shifting of emotions.
Blessed be this letting go of old hurts and pains.
Blessed be this reliable balancing act of nature.
Blessed be this rededication of values and meaning in
life.

Blessed be . . . [*add others*]
O Great Spirit of Hope, blessed be your holy seasons.

Reflection

What are the transitions that I experience as a new
season of a new year dawns?
What new goals for health, social change and
sharpening my focus do I set for myself?

[*Pause to reflect, journal, converse, draw or dance as you
wish.*]

Closing

This is the season of hope!
Let the Spirit of Hope surround you.
    Let your spirit rise to bless this new year.

[*Blow out the candle(s) knowing you can rekindle one or all
at any time.*
Happy New Year!]

Diann
L. Neu

125   **We shall go out**

We shall go out with hope of resurrection,
We shall go out, from strength to strength go on,
We shall go out and tell our stories boldly,
    Tales of a love that will not let us go.
We'll sing our songs of wrongs that can be righted,
We'll dream our dream of hurts that can be healed,
We'll weave a cloth of all the world united
    Within a vision of a Christ who sets us free.

Tune:

Londonderry Air,

Traditional Irish

We'll give a voice to those who have not spoken,
We'll find the words for those whose lips are sealed,
We'll make the tunes for those who sing no longer,
  Vibrating love alive in every heart.
We'll share our joy with those who are still weeping,
Chant hymns of strength for hearts that break in grief,
We'll leap and dance the resurrection story
  Including all within the circles of our love.

June

Boyce-Tillman

¹²⁶ Still centre

It is a still place where love is
and the way is very simple
it is so simple that I cannot understand
Jean   how hard it is to find the way
Clark   into the silence where love is

¹²⁷ And you held me

And you held me and there were no words
and there was no time and you held me
and there was only wanting and
being held and being filled with wanting
and I was nothing but letting go
and being held
and there were no words and there
needed to be no words
and there was no terror   only stillness
and I was wanting nothing and
it was fullness and it was like aching for God
and it was touch and warmth and
darkness and no time and no words and we flowed
and I flowed and I was not empty
and I was given up to the dark and
in the darkness   I was not lost
and the wanting was like fullness and I could
hardly hold it and I was held and
Janet   you were dark and warm and without time and
Morley   without words and you held me

¹²⁸ The bodies of grownups

The bodies of grownups
come with stretchmarks and scars,

faces that have been lived in,
relaxed breasts and bellies,
backs that give trouble,
and well-worn feet:
flesh that is particular,
and obviously mortal.
They also come
with bruises on their heart,
wounds they can't forget,
and each of them
a company of lovers in their soul
who will not return
and cannot be erased.
And yet I think there is a flood of beauty
beyond the smoothness of youth;
and my heart aches for that grace of longing
that flows through bodies
Janet no longer straining to be innocent,
Morley but yearning for redemption.

129   **Sing out my soul**

Sing out my soul,
sing of the holiness of God:
who has delighted in a woman,
lifted up the poor,
satisfied the hungry,
given voice to the silent,
grounded the oppressor,
blessed the full-bellied with emptiness,
and with the gift of tears
those who have never wept;
who has desired the darkness of the womb,
and inhabited our flesh.
Janet Sing of the longing of God,
Morley sing out, my soul.

130 **She comes with mother's kindnesses**

She comes with mother's kindnesses
And bends to touch and heal.
She gives her heart away in love
For those who cannot feel.

She comes with lover's tenderness
To answer love's appeal,
She gives her body with her heart
To make her passion real.

She comes with worker's faithfulness
To sow and reap and spin.
She bends her back in common task
To gather harvest in.

She comes with artist's joyfulness
To make and shape and sing,
She gives her hands and from them grow
A free and lovely thing.

She comes, a child in humbleness
And trust is in her eyes,
And through them all of life appears
In wondering surprise.

She comes with sister's carefulness,
Strong to support and bind,
Her voice will speak for justice' sake,
And peace is in her mind.

Tune: Martyrs   She comes with power like the night
And glory like the day,
Kathy   Her reign is in the heart of things,
Galloway   Oh come to us and stay.

131   **Dear Mother God**

Dear Mother God, your wings are warm around us,
We are enfolded in your love and care;
Safe in the dark, your heartbeat's pulse surrounds us,
You call to us, for you are always there.

You call to us, for we are in your image.
We wait on you, the nest is cold and bare –
High overhead your wingbeats call us onward.
Filled with your power, we ride the empty air.

Metre
11.10.11.10

Janet
Wootton

Let not our freedom scorn the needs of others –
We climb the clouds until our strong heart sings –
May we enfold our sisters and our brothers,
Till all are strong, till all have eagles' wings.

132   **Womanly God**

Prompted by an
article by Susan
Howdle, Vice-
President of the
Methodist Church
in Britain 1993-4,
in which she asked
why the only
female image of
God is as mother.

Womanly God, who are you?
The weaver of warm garments and magic tapestries;
The homemaker, welcoming and accepting;
The sister, second half – disturbingly other;
The listening, reassuring friend, silent consolation;
The delightful daughter, discovering and dancing;
The encouraging teacher, suggesting new words, new
        vision;
The backbreaking planter of fields, weeding, reaping;
        the treader of wine;
The nurse with full breasts and herbal remedies;
The virgin bride, the fulfilling wife, the desolate
        widow;
The free creative maiden; the long-living treasury of

Mary
Ann Ebert

        wisdom;
The wind that makes the heart sing.

133

133   O taste and see

Now is the time for the good wine
Pressed from the fruit of the tree
Now is the time for rejoicing
In the place where the feast will be
O taste and see
And refresh us with love.

Leave all the cares of the growing
Just let the mystery sing
Magic of ripening and pruning
And the fullness that time will bring
O taste and see
And refresh us with love.

Tune: Frankie and
Johnnie

Kathy
Galloway

Sweet-tasting cup of our loving
Promise of pleasure and pain
Take it and drink of it deeply
For the new life it will contain
O taste and see
And refresh us with love.

134   Song for love

Now we sing to praise love's blessing
All through our lives,
Laughter, joy, surprise confessing,
All through our lives.
Love that dreamed a new creation,
Love that dared an incarnation,
Love that offers transformation
All through our lives.

How our wounds ache for love's healing,
All through our days,
How our world needs love's revealing,
In all its ways.
Fearful hearts suspect the stranger,
Hardened nations arm for danger,
Love lives on, the powerful changer
All through our days.

Love's the grace that makes us caring
All through our lives,
Urges us to warmth and sharing,
All through our lives,
Speaks in us, oppression naming,
Strives in us, injustice shaming,
Lives in us, true peace proclaiming
All through our lives.

Love's the clown that mocks at winning,
All through the world,
Midwife of each new beginning,
All through the world.
In the struggles that confound us,
In the chaos all around us,
Love's wide arms with hope surround us
All through the world.

In God's faithful love we flourish
All through our lives,
Known and loved, each other nourish
All through our lives.
Though the world's demands are pressing,
What life brings is left to guessing,
Still we sing to praise love's blessing
All through our lives.

Tune: All through
the night

Anna
Briggs

135   Come down O love divine

Come down, O love divine,
Fulfil the promised time
When we on earth shall see that Second Coming.
O Comforter, draw near,
Within our world appear,
For all creation waits with eager longing.

Alas the hour is late –
The world awaits her fate
As life to dust and ashes we are turning.
Now nature's pattern breaks,
And poison fills her lakes,
The forests of the future we are burning.

Earth groans amid her chains,
Consumed by famine's pains;
The Beast defiles the face of God's creation.
Behold the horsemen four
Ride to the final war.
Now breaks the seal upon God's revelation.

Come, Holy Wisdom, down,
See now her twelve-starred crown –
Here is redeemed God's lovely spoiled creation.
O holy city, come!
Angela   Peace rules Jerusalem,
West   And all God's creatures share in Christ's salvation.

136   Amma of tenderness

Amma of tenderness,
    birth-giver
        source of my hope, my refreshment, my
           healing,
        source of all wisdom and beauty and longing:
      Spirit of transfiguration

revealed in the living
and giving
and rescue
of Jesus the Healer:
Draw me up from the pit of refusal
of false-learnt responses that look for
protection
from pain or from wholeness
seeking refuge in hollows
of unhallowed emptiness, gulping distraction,
chasing the shadows for fear of the light
of your love:
Draw me up from the lure of my gifting,
my dreaming,
my grasping.
Hold me, enfold me strongly and softly
in the arms of your mercy
till the turbulent echo
is stilled
to the answering heartbeat,
heart's ease,
trust,
joy at the heart of creation:
until all that is me
becomes focused
and free
in the wordless embrace
of encompassing grace.
Consummation.
Amma-mana-manna-maranatha.
Amen.

Brigid
Pailthorpe

137   **Celebration for deliverance from oppression**

Agape for South
London Industrial
Mission (February
1987).

For the promise to Sarah and Abraham that
the quest for the future is not futile:
Bless the Lord, all created things;

For God's tender compassion towards the enslaved:
Bless the Lord, you heavens;
For our deliverance from hopeless striving after
    individual salvation:
Bless the Lord you angels of the Lord;
For the might of God's arm, which lifts the people time
    and again into new faithfulness:
Bless the Lord all you his hosts;
For God's calling us to hunger and thirst after
    righteousness:
Sing God's praise and exalt the Lord for ever;
For our being as a community of women and men
    made in God's image:
O people of God bless the Lord;
Sing God's praise and exalt the Lord for ever;
Bless the Lord all people of upright spirit,
Bless the Lord you that are holy and humble in heart.

Alison   Bless God, Creator, Redeemer, Lover,
Norris   Sing God's praise and exalt the Lord for ever.

138   **Praise to God, the world's creator**

Praise to God, the world's creator,
    Source of life and growth and breath,
Cradling in her arms her children,
    Holding them from birth to death.
In our bodies, in our living,
    Strength and truth of all we do,
God is present, working with us,
    Making us creators too.

Praise to God, our saving Wisdom,
    Meeting us with love and grace,
Helping us to grow in wholeness,
    Giving freedom, room, and space.
In our hurting, in our risking,
    In the thoughts we dare not name,
God is present, growing with us,
    Healing us from sin and shame.

Tune: Abbot's
Leigh

Praise to God, the Spirit in us,
> Prompting hidden depths of prayer,
Firing us to long for justice,
> Reaching out with tender care.
In our searching, in our loving,
> In our struggles to be free,
God is present, living in us,
> Pointing us to what shall be.

Jan
Berry

¹³⁹   **A confession of faith**

We believe in God,
> Maker, Redeemer and Sustainer of Life,
> without beginning or end,
> whose life-giving love was let loose on the first
> Easter Sunday
> and whose life-giving love we share and proclaim
> here today.

We believe in God
> who gave up the divine life and
> submitted to the darkness and terror of the grave;
> and who enters with us unto every darkness and
> terror
> we shall ever face.

We believe in God
> who raised Christ from the death of the grave to
> glorious new life;
> and who raises our lives from sin and despair
> to newness and hope again.

We believe in God
> who met the grief-stricken Mary in the garden
> and called her into hope by the uttering of her
> name;

and who meets us in our grief and gives us
    courage to hope again
by tenderly calling our name.

We believe in God
    who sent Mary out from the garden
    to be the witness and apostle of the resurrection;
    and who commissions, like Mary,
    to be bearers of hope and good news in our
        world.

We believe in God
    Maker, Redeemer and Sustainer of Life,
    without beginning or end,
    whose life-giving love was let loose on the first
      Easter Sunday
    and whose life-giving love we share and proclaim
      today
    to all women and men, wherever and whoever
      they are,

Nicola   loved, blessed and called by God,
Slee   without beginning or end.

140   Psalm

I will praise God, my Beloved,
for she is altogether lovely.

Her presence satisfies my soul;
she fills my senses to overflowing
so that I cannot speak.

Her touch brings me to life;
the warmth of her hands makes me wholly alive.

Her embrace nourishes me, body and spirit;
every part of my being responds to her touch.

The beauty of her face is more than I can bear;
in her gaze I drown.

When she looks upon me
I can withhold nothing;

When she asks for my love
all my defences crumble;
my pride and my control are utterly dissolved.

O God I fear your terrible mercy;
I am afraid to surrender my self.

If I let go into the whirlpool of your love,
shall I survive the embrace?

If I fall into the strong currents of your desire
shall I escape drowning?

But how shall I refuse my Beloved,
and how can I withdraw from the one my heart yearns
      for?

On the edge of your abyss I look down and I tremble;
but I will not stand gazing for ever.

Even in chaos you will bear me up;
if the waters go over my head,
you will still be holding me.

For the chaos is yours also,
and in the swirling of mighty waters
is your presence known.

If I trust her, surely her power will not fail me;
nor will she let me be utterly destroyed.

Though I lose all knowledge and all security,
yet will my God never forsake me;

But she will recreate me, in her steadfast love,
so that I need not be afraid.

Janet
Morley
Then will I praise my Beloved among the people,
among those who seek to know God.

141   Jubilee hymn

('The day of resurrection' – re-written)

The day of Jubilation,
Earth tell it out abroad!
The Jubilee of justice,
The Jubilee of God!
From debt to equal living,
From sickness unto health,
Our Christ has purchased Jubilee
Of Earth's abundant wealth.

Our hearts be free from envy,
That we may see again
Our sisters and our brothers
Freed from their agelong pain.
Let hunger now be banished,
And all who thirst drink deep;
So may we sing and praise the Lord,
Our Jubilee to keep.

Now let the heavens be joyful,
Let earth her song begin,
The round world keep high triumph,
And all that is therein;
Let all things seen and unseen
Their notes of gladness blend,
Alison
Norris
For Jubilee is come again,
God's justice without end.

142 **Benedicite omnia opera**

This canticle was
first used at the
Greenham vigil,
August 1987.

All you works of God, bless your creator;
praise her and glorify her for ever.

Let the wide earth bless the creator;
let the arching heavens bless the creator;
let the whole body of God bless the creator;
praise her and glorify her for ever.

You returning daylight, bless your creator;
twilight and shadows, bless your creator;
embracing darkness, bless your creator;
praise her and glorify her for ever.

Mountains of God, massive and ancient rocks, bless
        your creator;
valleys and pastures, moorland and rivers, bless your
        creator;
ocean depths and lonely abyss, bless your creator;
praise her and glorify her for ever.

Storm and mighty wind, bless your creator;
bitter cold and scorching sun, bless your creator;
mist and cloud and tender rain, bless your creator;
praise her and glorify her for ever.

Seed and sapling, tree and vivid flower, bless your
        creator;
greenness and flourishing, withering and barrenness,
        bless your creator;
harvest and springtime and deadness of the year, bless
        your creator,
praise her and glorify her for ever.

You creatures of God, bless your creator;
swift and cunning, violent and graceful, bless your
        creator;

all who creep and soar and dance across the earth, bless
    your creator;
praise her and glorify her for ever.

You newborn babies, bless your creator;
young and old, mature and ageing, bless your creator;
all you dying, bless your creator;
praise her and glorify her for ever.

In pain and desolation, let us bless our creator;
in the place of delight, let us bless our creator;
in time of waiting, let us bless our creator;
praise her and glorify her for ever.

Let all who live and grow and breathe bless our
Janet   creator,
Morley **praise her and glorify her for ever.**

143 An Easter prayer

Christ our life,
you are alive   in the beauty of the earth
             in the rhythm of the seasons
             in the mystery of time and space
             Alleluia

Christ our life,
you are alive   in the tenderness of touch
             in the heartbeat of intimacy
             in the insights of solitude
             Alleluia

Christ our life,
you are alive   in the creative possibility
             of the dullest conversation
             the dreariest task
             the most threatening event
             Alleluia

Christ our life,
you are alive   to offer re-creation
             to every unhealed hurt

to every deadened place
to every damaged heart
Alleluia.

You set before us a great choice.
Therefore we choose life.
The dance of resurrection soars and surges through
    the whole creation.
It sets gifts of bread and wine upon our table.

Kathy   This is grace, dying we live.
Galloway   So let us live.

144   Eternal God, as you created humankind
in your image, women and men, male and female,
renew us in that image;
God, the Holy Spirit, by your strength and
love comfort us as those whom a mother
      comforts;
Lord Jesus Christ, by your death and resurrection,
give us the joy of those for whom pain and suffering
become, in hope, the fruitful agony of travail;
God, the Holy Trinity, grant that we may together
enter into a new life, your promised rest of
achievement and fulfilment – world without
      end.
Amen.

145   Tender God, touch us.
Be touched by us;
make us lovers of humanity,
compassionate friends of all creation.
Gracious God, hear us into speech;
speak us into acting;

Carter   and through us, recreate the world.
Heyward   **Amen.**

146   The blessing of the God of Sarah and Hagar,
as of Abraham,
the blessing of the Son, born of the
      woman Mary,
the blessing of the Holy Spirit
      who broods over us

Lois   as a mother, her children,
Wilson   be with you all. **Amen.**

147   The blessing of the most holy Trinity
           God unbegotten
           God incarnate
           God among us
       Keep us now and for evermore.
       Amen.

148   **Romans 8.14–17**

       God, give us our share of the inheritance.
       Give us the doubt in the wilderness,
       and the power to heal.
       Give us the vision of the Kingdom,
       and the ability to tell stories.
       Give us a raging hunger for justice,
       and the need to be touched.
       Give us our inheritance.
       Give us the life of Christ,
Alison   through his death and resurrection.
Norris   **Amen.**

149   **Self-offering in preparation for priesthood**

       Shape me for your service:
       Pin back my arms
       That I might proclaim freedom
       To a captive world.

       Teach me by your wisdom:
       Unfold your word
       That I might share truth
       With a hungry people.

       Hold me in your love:
       Nurse my need

Jane That I might tender healing
Tillier For a broken body.

150   **Prayer during a child's confirmation**

('Cwch' is a
particularly Welsh
word – 'cuddle' or   May God stride out before you on your journey
'snuggle' nearly   through life
does the same.   and through prayer.
'Hold' would do
but sounds much   May Jesus, your playful brother,
colder.)   pace you in his holy way to the end.

Siân
Swain   May the Holy Spirit greet you at
Taylor   each corner and cwch you to her breast.

151   **Blessing for a pregnant woman**

May our Mother God keep you safe until the time of
    your deliverance.
May you, and those eagerly awaiting your 'hour' be
    enfolded in peace.
May our God of patient waiting be your strength
    during these days of anticipation.
May our Midwife God protect and comfort you during
    your labour.
May our God of love and life transform your labour
    pains into joy, in the gift of a healthy child.
May our Nurturing Mother God provide you with an
    abundance of milk, to nourish your newborn
    infant.
And may the blessing of the God who conceived us
with joy, birthed us in pain, and transforms us in
love, to fullness of life and fruitfulness; may this
Maria   God bless you, and keep you in her womanly
Kersten   tenderness today and always.   **Amen**.

152 Easter blessing

May the God who shakes heaven and earth,
whom death could not contain,
who lives to disturb and heal us,
bless you with power to go forth
Janet   and proclaim the gospel.
Morley   **Amen.**

153 'Down and not up, in and not out'

God the ground of all being,
hold us in the depths of your love,
take us deep into the heart of your covenant,
Alison   and let your blessing go with us now.
Norris   **Amen.**

154 Wisdom blessing

Blessing adapted   May Wisdom be in our minds, and in our thinking;
from Sarum   May Wisdom be in our hearts, and in our perceiving;
Primer   May Wisdom be in our mouths, and in our speaking;
Benediction,   May Wisdom be in our hands, and in our working;
1636.   May Wisdom be in our feet, and in our walking;
Diann   May Wisdom be in our bodies, and in our loving;
L. Neu   May Wisdom be with us all the days of our lives.

155 Blessing Song

May the blessing of God go before you.
May her grace and peace abound.
May her spirit live within you.
Miriam   May her love wrap you round.
Therese   May her blessing remain with you always.
Winter   May you walk on holy ground. **Amen.**

¹⁵⁶ **Sending forth**

May peace be within us.
May peace be around us.
May peace be beside us.
May peace be between us.
May we walk peacefully with Mother Earth.
May peace fill our days and our nights.
May peace fill the earth. Amen. Blessed be.
  Let it be so.

*Diann
L. Neu*

¹⁵⁷ **Mother of infinite wisdom**

Mother of infinite wisdom,
Christ of infinite compassion,
Holy Spirit, guarantee of change,
bring us to our knees in shame,
bring us to our feet in action,
bring us to our senses in prayer,
that with you we may all inherit
a new heaven and a new earth.

*Kate
McIlhagga*

¹⁵⁸ **Flight into Egypt: a benediction**

Our brother Jesus, you set our feet upon the way
      and sometimes where you lead we do not like or
      understand.
Bless us with courage where the way is fraught with
      dread or danger;
Bless us with graceful meetings where the way is
      lonely;
Bless us with good companions where the way demands
      a common cause;
Bless us with night vision where we travel in the dark,
      keen hearing where we have not sight, to hear the
      reassuring sounds of fellow travellers,

Bless us with humour – we cannot travel lightly
  weighed down with gravity;
Bless us with humility to learn from those around us;
Bless us with decisiveness where we must move with
  speed;
Bless us with lazy moments, to stretch and rest and
  savour;
Bless us with love, given and received;
And bless us with your presence, even when we know
  it in your absence.
Lead us into exile,
until we find that on the road
is where you are,
and where you are is going home.

Kathy Bless us, lead us, love us, bring us home
Galloway bearing the gospel of life.

¹⁵⁹ **Post-Communion prayer**

  All: Living God, we thank you that in this
     sacrament you make yourself known to us.
    From now on, whenever we walk in strange
     places, we shall find your footprints there;
    whenever we meet with unknown faces, we
     shall see your image there;
    whenever we face nameless terror we shall hear
     your 'Fear not' there;
    whenever we stumble into unexpected joy, we
     shall feel your heartbeat there.

  Celebrant:

Alison   Wherever we go we start from here;
Norris   Go in the peace of Christ.

160 **Gathered together**

As we indicated in the introduction we hope that this book will not only be a resource but will also be an encouragement to women to plan and write their own worship material. What we have done in this section, therefore, is to share some thoughts and suggestions from our own and others' experience of what affects the quality of our worship together. They are offered as practical hints rather than definitive guidelines!

Silence

Because this is essentially a book of words, the first thing to acknowledge is that there are other ways of communicating with one another and of expressing our search for the beyond. Most of us spend our lives rushing from one activity to another and the last thing we need when we gather for worship is the same lack of breathing space for our souls. The following points are useful to bear in mind when including silence:

1. The words we use are sometimes very powerful, for example, hearing God referred to for the first time as Mother, Sister, Lover; we need time to digest what we hear and allow it to touch us. Silence after readings is important.

2. Shared silence is an intimate experience and one that cannot be entered into lightly. Most of us are not very used to silence and we need 'permission' to be silent. Make sure that people know how long the silence will last, that it is a time of silence, and make its beginning and end clear.

Symbols

Another important medium of expression in worship is the use of various kinds of symbols. These may be material objects like bread and wine, a pebble or a leaf, or they may be symbolic gestures. We have given

some examples below and have found the following
general points helpful:

1. Symbols should emerge from the readings and
prayers which form other parts of the act of worship. If
it is a group which meets regularly, ideally symbols
will arise from the ongoing life of the group itself. The
meaning of the symbol needs to be a shared one.

2. If you are asking a group to participate in a symbolic
gesture (e.g. anointing) it is helpful to give them a
specific phrase to repeat as they do it. If you want the
gesture to be done in silence, say so, in order to avoid
a sense of unease or embarrassment.

3. Symbolic objects have a material history. For
example, using a symbolic food from a country whose
labourers are severely exploited as part of a celebratory
agape seems contradictory.

4. Use what is around, either in a material sense (e.g.
lighting candles from an open fire) or in a seasonal one.
Exploring the theme of darkness in the summer months
can have its problems!

Bodies

The body has had a hard time in the Christian tradition
and it is important that we learn to affirm our bodies,
not least in the part they play in worship. Bodies, too,
are symbols: we make symbolic gestures with them and
where we place them to worship may say more than
the words we use. For instance, the words of the
Wilderness Liturgy (p. 109) had a much more intense
meaning when those who said them placed themselves
physically outside the church building. Also, words like
'sin', 'salvation', 'crucifixion', 'Lord', mean quite different
things when you say them standing at the perimeter
fence at Greenham Common than they do recited in
Westminster Abbey.

As well as using our bodies to make political statements
we can also enjoy them in our worship. You will notice
that we have suggested the use of warm, scented water

for foot/hand washing, simply because it feels and smells good.

Tradition

As well as using what is around us in a physical sense we can also use what there is in the tradition, making women's experience in the tradition more visible: for example, celebrating particular days of the liturgical year like the Visitation and Annunciation, or the days of women saints, both old and new.

General points

1. Worship needs planning and it is good for at least two people to do this together.
2. Make sure everyone can participate in the worship – share leadership, readings, prayers, etc.
3. Leave some space for spontaneity.
4. Include a variety of different elements and types of material – silence, singing, readings, prayers, sharing reflections, etc.
5. Despite traditional church pews, there doesn't seem to be anything to be gained by being uncomfortable. Make the space you choose for worship as physically comfortable as you can.
6. Finally, try to make sure that the worship does not feel separate from the rest of life. Several things can help this:
– worshipping in people's homes;
– including a meal as part of the worship;
– allowing time before and after the worship for participants to chat together.

Some examples

Here are a few examples of the way in which the theme of an act of worship can be linked through a reading, a shared symbolic gesture, and a greeting or affirmation. These are all ideas that have been tried:

1. *Theme:* Women affirm each other's vision.
   Reading: Luke 1.39–56: The visit of Mary to Elizabeth.
   Action: A hug for each person in the room, or, if there are large numbers, for the people nearby.
   Greeting: Blessed are you among women.

2. *Theme:* Touch, acceptability, tenderness.
   Reading: Luke 7.36–50 or John 12.1–8: A woman anoints Jesus' feet.
   Action: Participants in turn wash one another's feet (or hands if preferred) around the circle. Use a bowl of warm water, scented with bath oil. (This is pleasant and removes the need for soap, which is inconvenient to handle.)
   Greeting: The process is not one that can be rushed or fitted to a phrase, so it is best to concentrate on doing the action lovingly. No particular words are necessary.

3: *Theme:* Preparation for mission/action.
   Reading: Mark 14.1–11 or Matthew 26.3–16: A woman anoints Jesus' head.
   Action: Use oil of lavender (or similar) in a small dish. Dip a finger or thumb in the perfume, and anoint the forehead of the next woman around the circle, making the sign of the cross.
   Greeting: . . . [Name] go forth and proclaim the gospel.

4. *Theme:* Darkness and light (e.g. in Advent).
   Reading: Psalm 139.
   Action: To introduce shared intercessions, the room is in darkness except for a fire in the hearth. Anyone who wants to make an intercession picks up a candle and lights it from the hearth, saying: 'I light this candle for . . .'.

¹⁶¹ **Nanjing Pentecost**

International
consultation in
Nanjing, China,
'Ecumenical
Sharing – A New
Agenda', May
1986.

Woman whose work is words
what will you do when words are
gone?
> Grow in silence like the trees
> find strength in solitude
> listen to wind, water and living things
> hear what God speaks in silence.

Woman who lives by words
what will you do when words are
strange?
> Listen for a change
> learn what people mean in other ways
> smile, gesture – weep even –
> live with questions and powerlessness.

Woman who cares for words
what will you do when words
overwhelm?
> Laugh at jargon, be angry
> when talk and papers oppress people –
> care more for them, remember
> the first and last Word that makes us one.

*Jan
Sutch
Pickard*

Acknowledgements

We wish to thank all those women who have contributed to this collection and given permission for their writing to be used.

We have made every effort to trace and identify pieces correctly, and to secure the necessary permission for printing. If we have made any errors in text or in acknowledgement, we apologize sincerely. The copyright for most pieces remains with the authors concerned. Please address the author, c/o SPCK, Holy Trinity Church, Marylebone Road, London, NW1 4DU for permission to reproduce, marking the envelope clearly: PERMISSIONS: CELEBRATING WOMEN. For items marked with an asterisk, permission should be sought from the publisher or agent specified.

These pieces or extracts first appeared as follows:

*Epigraph: extract from Dorothy L. Sayers, 'The Human-Not-Quite-Human' in *Unpopular Opinions* (Gollancz 1946), reprinted by permission of David Higham Associates Ltd.

'Come to the living God', 'God of the poor', 'The desert', 'Roll back the stone', 'Lent', 'We call them wise', 'Christmas', 'Epiphany' and 'She comes with mother's kindnesses' in Janet Morley (ed.), *Bread of Tomorrow* (Christian Aid/SPCK 1992).

'Meditation with silence' and 'Clear the way' in Edmund Banyard (ed.), *All Year Round* (CCBI 1992).

'Spirit of God' and 'Mother of infinite wisdom' in Kate Compston (ed.), *Encompassing Presence* (United Reformed Church 1993).

'Spirit of comfort and longing', 'Prayer at a funeral', 'New collects', 'The remembrance of them', 'Eucharistic prayer for Christmas Eve', 'That night we gathered', 'And you held me', 'The bodies of grownups', 'Sing out my soul', 'Benedicite omnia opera' and 'Easter blessing' in Janet Morley, *All Desires Known*

(Women in Theology/Movement for the Ordination of Women 1988, and SPCK (expanded edition) 1992); reproduced by permission of SPCK.

'A story of creation' in Jean C. Morrison (ed.), *What on Earth is God Like?* (Wild Goose Publications 1985).

'The other' in Diana Scott (ed.), *Bread and Roses* (Virago Press 1982).

'Out of the depths', 'In love revealed', and 'We lay our broken world' in *Women's Words from Iona Abbey* (Wild Goose Publications 1985).

'Bed and breakfast' in Ann Lewin, *Between the Lines* (Ann Lewin 1988), now available in *Candles and Kingfishers* (1993).

*'The Crack' in Kathy Galloway, *Struggles to Love* (SPCK 1994), reproduced by permission of SPCK.

'Litany for many voices' in *Vashti's Voice*, No. 10 (1981).

'Broken Silence' in *Broken Silence: Women Finding a Voice* (Women in Theology 1993).

'Wachet Auf' and 'Revelation' in Ann Lewin, *Unfinished Sentences* (Ann Lewin 1987), now available in *Candles and Kingfishers* (1993).

'Merry Christmas' and 'Acceptable losses' in Ann Lewin, *Candles and Kingfishers* (Ann Lewin 1993).

'The guest' in *NOW* magazine (Methodist Church Overseas Division 1982).

'Just a housewife' in Belper Writers' Group, *Mini-Tales* (1992).

'In the house of Simon the leper', occasional paper (Gay Christian Movement 1982).

'Pieta' in *Oceans of Prayer* (NCEC 1991).

'"Woman, why are you weeping?"' in Rosemary Neave (ed.), *Gossiping the Gospel: Women Reflect on Evangelism* (Auckland, The Women's Resource Centre, 1991).

'Let us now praise noble women' in *Vashti's Voice*, No. 4 (1979).

'The sharing' in Edwina Gateley, *Psalms of a laywoman* (Claretian Publications 1981).

'Litany' and 'The way of forgiveness' in Michael Hare Duke (ed.), *Praying for peace: Reflections of the Gulf*

Crisis (HarperCollins Fount 1991); reproduced with permission.

*'God of justice and peace' and 'The blessing of the most holy Trinity' are adapted from 'The Women's Agape', devised from the early Christian *Didache* by Liz Campbell, in *Greenham Vigil Office*, © Greenham Peace Vigil 1986.

'Re-igniting fires of justice' in *WATERwheel*, Vol. 5, No. 1, Spring 1992 (Women's Alliance for Theology, Ethics and Ritual).

'Hymn for Transition House Sunday' was published by the United Church, Atlantic Provinces, Canada, for use on 'Transition House' Sundays.

'From women in ministry' in *Chrysalis*, July 1993 (Movement for the Ordination of Women).

'Prayer' in *Novena* (Movement for the Ordination of Women 1992).

'Blessing the bread' and 'The blessing of the God of Sarah and Hagar' in Iben Gjerding and Katherine Kinnamon (eds.), *No Longer Strangers* (WCC 1983).

'Blessing of bread', 'Blessing of fruit of the vine' and 'Sending forth' in *WATERwheel*, Vol. 3 No. 3, Fall 1990 (Women's Alliance for Theology, Ethics and Ritual).

'Feast of life' in *International Review of Mission*, October 1982.

'Did the woman say?' in *National Catholic Reporter*, 21 December 1979, reprinted by permission of the author and of National Catholic Reporter, PO Box 410281, Kansas City, MO 64141.

'Wrestler' in the Julian magazine, Summer 1989.

'On leaving the church' in *Women-Church*, 6, Autumn 1990.

'I am a woman' in Hong Kong Women Christian Council Newsletter, April 1992.

*'We shall go out' and 'Dear Mother God' in June Boyce-Tillman and Janet Wootton (eds.), *Reflecting Praise* (Stainer & Bell/Women In Theology 1993), reproduced by permission of Stainer & Bell and Women In Theology.

'A confession of faith' in The St Hilda Community, *Women Included* (SPCK 1991), reproduced by permission of SPCK.

'Eternal God, as you created humankind' in 'The Letter to Sheffield', Community of Women and Men in the Church – Sheffield Report (WCC 1983), by permission of the World Council of Churches.

'Wisdom blessing' in *WATERwheel* Vol. 6, No. 3, Fall 1993 (Women's Alliance for Theology, Ethics and Ritual).

*'Blessing song' in Miriam Therese Winter, *WomanPrayer, WomanSong* (Meyer Stone/Crossroad 1987); © Medical Mission Sisters 1987.

*'Naming and presentation' and 'Flight into Egypt: a benediction' in *Coracle* 3/11, © Iona Community 1992.

Index of contributors (*numbers refer to items*)

Index of titles or first lines *(numbers refer to items)*